WILLIAM BEARDMORE
'Transport is the Thing'

THE WIDE RANGE OF
VEHICLES, AIRCRAFT,
MOTORCYCLES, *etc*
PRODUCED BY
WILLIAM BEARDMORE & COMPANY LTD

K. A. HURST

MI MechE(SA)

NATIONAL MUSEUMS OF SCOTLAND

Published by NMSE Publishing
a division of NMS Enterprises Limited
National Museums of Scotland
Chambers Street
Edinburgh EH1 1JF

ISBN 1-901663-53-1

British Library Cataloguing in Publication Data
A catalogue record of this book
is available from the British Library.

Design by NMS Enterprises Limited – Publishing.
Printed by Athenaeum Press, Gateshead, Tyne & Wear.

Cover images: William Beardmore courtesy of Glasgow University Archives;
others courtesy of the Museum of Flight and the Mitchell Library.

CONTENTS

*To my father
whose guidance and enthusiasm
helped me to achieve my ambition
to become an engineer.*

This work is published with the assistance of the Michael Sedgwick Memorial Trust. Founded in memory of the famous motoring researcher and author Michael Sedgwick (1926–83), the Trust is a registered charity to encourage new research and recording of motoring history.

Suggestions for future projects, and donations, should be sent to the Honorary Secretary of the Michael Sedgwick Memorial Trust, c/o the John Montagu Building, Beaulieu, Hampshire SO41 7ZN, United Kingdom.

PREFACE

IN a book such as this, a great deal of research has to be undertaken before any words can be written. The task of carrying out such research has been complicated by the fact that I live in South Africa and the major source of information is in Scotland. A further difficulty lies in the fact that most of the Beardmore company records were donated to a paper salvage drive during World War II. With one or two exceptions (one factory manufactures wellington boots, the other produces eggs), all the factories comprising the Beardmore industrial empire have been bulldozed to make way for other activities; virtually nothing of this once great enterprise now exists, and those surviving vehicles produced during its lifetime are few and far between.

On the plus side I have one big advantage. I had a father who was manager of Beardmore's Parkhead Forge, and as a small boy I remember being taken on visits to most of the Beardmore factories, where I met many of the people mentioned in this book.

In order to fill in gaps a certain amount of circumstantial evidence has had to be accepted. If, in the search for the truth of what happened and why it happened in the way it did, the stature of any of those personalities involved appears to have been diminished, it was not the objective of this book to do so.

As the incompetence of the Military and Naval High Commands during the same period has been well documented, it should come as no surprise that many of their civilian counterparts, the 'Captains of Industry', were tarred with the same brush. If it is any consolation, then some of the biggest blunders – military, political, economic, industrial, *etc* – have been committed by the nicest of people.

Without the help of Flight Lieutenant Charles E. Mackay this work could not have been undertaken. Charles carried out an enormous amount of research for me and provided a great deal of raw material. His wide knowledge of Beardmore and other aero engines has been, to say the least, invaluable.

I have had extensive correspondence with people all over the world. The majority of them replied to my letters and were of the utmost help. In particular I would like to thank the following: Mr R. J. Davies, managing director of Fletcher Smith Ltd (Duncan Stewart); Mr A. B. Demaus (1908

5

Humber TT Cars); Mr David McIvor (for details of his 1924 two-litre Beardmore Super Sports, and information on Beardmore commercial vehicles); Mr Michael S. Moss, archivist at Glasgow University (for permission to quote from his books *Beardmore, The History of a Scottish Industrial Giant* and *The Bitter with the Sweet*). Also the late Mr Brian Porter (for details of his 1912 15.9 Arrol-Johnston Tourer and Mr Dicken Daggert, a later owner of the car); Mr Graham Thomas (for photographs and details of his 1924 12/30 Beardmore Tourer); Mr Chris Tait (Dunelt); Mr Brian West (Beardmore Taxicabs Ltd); and Mr Peter Kimberley (for photographs of his Taxi Mk VI, the last to be made at Paisley).

Of great assistance were the Glasgow Museum of Transport, the Glasgow University Archives, the National Motor Museum, the Royal Airforce Museum, the Scottish Records Office, and the Tank Museum.

Kenneth A. Hurst MI MechE(SA)
SOUTH AFRICA

AUTHOR'S NOTE

WILLIAM Beardmore became a baronet in 1914 and Lord Invernairn in 1921. In this history, for the sake of simplicity, he is referred to as 'William Beardmore' or 'Beardmore' throughout.

THE RISE OF WILLIAM BEARDMORE & COMPANY LTD

Rise to eminence of William Beardmore & Company Ltd – dealings with Thornycroft and Vickers – investment in Arrol-Johnston

AT the turn of the twentieth century William Beardmore made a considerable impact on the Scottish engineering industry and it is almost impossible to separate his various enterprises. He was involved in the ship propulsion business that had developed from steam to high-speed diesel engines. This was linked to the aero engine business which produced engines for the, tragically, disastrous R101 airship. Aero engines, involving Dr Ing Ferdinand Porsche, also had some indirect influence on both Arrol-Johnston and Beardmore cars, which in turn had links with the taxi business and motorcycle industry. At the same time, there was an association with Fiat, licensors of the Caprotti-valve gear for steam engines, which provided the designs for the Galloway car.

The Beardmore industrial empire began with William's grandfather in 1815. It developed to include steelmaking, heavy forgings, rolling mills, armour plate, naval guns, battleships, passenger liners, marine diesels (built under licence from Tosi of Italy – the sort you have to climb two flights of stairs just to adjust the tappets), aircraft, airships (the R34 was the first airship to carry out a double crossing of the Atlantic in 1919), aero engines, high-speed diesel engines, steam locomotives, six separate cars, four different makes of commercial vehicles, and two different motorcycle and motorcycle engine companies in ten different factories. There was even an attempt around 1924 to produce compressed board, a forerunner to the plastics industry.

Rudder Frame, Parkhead Forge

Beardmore was an ambitious entrepreneur and expansionist. After World War I legend has it that he summed up his peacetime strategy with the simple sentence: 'Transport is the thing.' Unfortunately, almost everyone with spare machine shop capacity had the same idea. Beardmore, however, planned his business on a large scale, building transport for land, sea and air. However, in doing this, he dissipated his resources.

Both the Rudder Frame (page 7) and the 3 Throw Crankshaft were made at Parkhead Forge, of which the author's father was manager. The Crankshaft was made for a steam driven Rolling Mill Engine, but was generally similar to marine propulsion units. The man who posed in front of the crankshaft was called 'Shorty'.

With hindsight it is easy to see what and where it all went wrong, and it must be remembered that since then the art of business management has progressed at a rate equal to the advances of technology.

In the post-World War I years, however, the workforce was made up of individual craftsmen. Son followed father, working at the same job for the same employer. Knowledge and skills were jealously guarded. Accountancy was not a tool of management at that time. Few factory managers knew how they stood financially on a monthly basis, and some only knew at the end of each year. The post of production engineer had not yet appeared and any market research generally reflected the personal prejudices of the sales director. Many managing directors owed their position as much to inheritance as ability and administered their responsibilities with a paternal despotism. A *laissez-faire* muddled thinking, combined with lack of communication and sometimes downright bad engineering, was not unusual.

It is said that in the thick of battle the side that makes the least number of mistakes wins. Beardmore may have had many pioneering successes, but all too often he made serious mistakes both in the engineering field and administration. He was a great innovator, but lacked the technical knowledge to discriminate between a genuine engineering advance and a mechanical curiosity. Thus many problems were due to his own shortcomings. Nick Morgan, a historian of the Glasgow scene, described Beardmore as 'a man whose enormous vision and imagination were probably only matched by his poverty of judgement and lack of business skills'. He was unable to delegate responsibility. He interfered with the day-to-day management of the business and, when faced with a financial loss, he simply borrowed more money.

In fairness Beardmore was also victim of circumstances over which he had no control: in particular, the great Depression which began in the

1920s. The effects were particularly severe for the shipbuilding, locomotive, steelmaking and armaments industries which made up the heart of the Beardmore empire. In an expanding economy it might have been a very different story.

William Beardmore's early achievements were spectacular nonetheless. His patriotism was enormous and during World War I he rushed into the production of armaments. His maxim was to produce the goods now and worry about payment later, but such impetuosity was not always rewarded, particularly when entrepreneurial energy exceeded administrative ability.

Beardmore's ties with other businesses are well known. Both he and his company were closely linked by financial and family connections to the Glasgow engineering firm of Duncan Stewart Ltd. William and his brother Joseph were large shareholders in the company, and their sister Marie was married to Duncan Stewart.

In 1899 Beardmore took over the bankrupt shipbuilding firm of Robert Napier and Sons and started on the construction of a large engineering and shipbuilding works at Dalmuir. At this juncture the Thames-based company of J. L. Thornycroft came onto the market due to the death of one of the partners, John Donaldson. Thornycroft was under an obligation to purchase Donaldson's shares, but was unable to do so without financial re-structuring. Thus a new company was formed with Beardmore as chairman.

The stake in the Thornycroft company gave Beardmore access to valuable technology, as well as a market for his products. He was already involved in the supply of parts to the emerging Scottish automobile industry. In 1902 Beardmore became a shareholder in the New Arrol-Johnston Car Company Ltd, and by 1905 he was the largest single shareholder. At the same time he purchased the controlling shares in Duncan Stewart Ltd. It is not really surprising that Beardmore ran out of cash.

Following the example of Thornycroft, Beardmore formed a limited liability company, probably in 1905, with a view to raising funds by selling a large part of the equity. With the help of London financiers Sir Ernest Cassel and Lord Rothschild, an amalgamation was carried out with Vickers, who themselves had just amalgamated with gun manufacturers Maxim and Nordenfeldt. The Vickers agreement opened up further opportunities for Beardmore in the form of armaments and Krupp Armour plate patents controlled by Vickers.

The agreement reached between Beardmore and Vickers was important and ultimately decided the fate of William Beardmore & Company Ltd. In the beginning, however, Vickers had a controlling interest in Beardmore, although later this was shared. Beardmore in turn become a director of Vickers Sons & Maxim Ltd, but Vickers subsidiaries were excluded (as were Arrol-Johnston and Duncan Stewart). However, the shares of J. L. Thornycroft were managed by the new company over which Vickers exercised control.

Beardmore already presided over a sizeable armaments business, having supplied field guns to the British Army and ships to the Admiralty during the Boer War. However, as a result of his association with Vickers, he expanded the armaments side of his business, putting in rolling mills for armour plate and machine shops and forges for the manufacture of guns.

Despite everything, William Beardmore & Company Ltd was not a great success and cash flow remained a problem throughout the company's existence. The large amount of money poured into creating the largest shipbuilding yard on the Clyde, plus the in-house supply of steam boilers, marine propulsion units, rolled and forged armour plate, naval guns, gun mountings and all the other accessories, called for a very high workload in order to achieve profitability. The expansion had been grossly over-extended and the company seldom achieved the necessary levels of orders.

Beardmore also started manufacturing aero engines under Austro Daimler licence, and aircraft under agreement with Deutsche Flugzenge Werke. He even established a carpentry and joinery factory for the manufacture of ships' bridges, wooden hatches *etc*, and another factory to produce furniture, staircases and panelling for passenger liners. When these items were not required the employees were laid off, but what could not be laid off were the overheads on buildings and the financial returns on expensive but idle machinery. Part of the situation was solved during World War I when the wood-working shops were employed in the manufacture of aircraft wings and fuselages.

Beardmore's association with Vickers also had a downside – it meant that Vickers knew the state of Beardmore's order book and the prices quoted for new contracts. Vickers even entered into secret talks with the Admiralty with the intention of excluding Beardmore from receiving contracts for the manufacture of submarines. Beardmore never managed to achieve the cosy relationship with the Admiralty, War Office and Air Ministry that Vickers established. Glasgow High School may have had higher educational standards, but it lacked the elitism of Eton, Harrow, Winchester, and so on. The 'Old Boy' network was not easily breached, and no doubt Vickers did their best to keep it that way.

Apart from Thornycroft's expertise in Torpedo boat destroyers, they also specialised in building steam carriages to their own patents, although financial problems prevented Beardmore from completing the full deal with Thorny-croft. Nevertheless, the Stewart-Thornycroft steam tractor was launched in 1903, and in 1909 Beardmore entered a Stewart steam wagon based on Thornycroft patents for War Office trials. Ironically the trials were won by Thornycroft using an internal combustion engine. Nevertheless, Beardmore went ahead with his plans to manufacture the machine under licence.

THE STEWART-THORNYCROFT
STEAM WAGON

The Stewart-Thornycroft steam wagon –
London Road Ironworks

THE original wagon was designated the 'Stewart-Thornycroft'. Rated at five tons at the draw bar and with an attachment for a trailer, the engine was a double-acting compound with cylinder bores of five and seven inches with an eight-inch stroke. Steam was supplied by a locomotive-type boiler at 175 pounds per square inch (psi). At 375 revolutions per minute (rev/min), the engine developed 40 brake horsepower (bhp) and 45bhp at 450 rev/min. Transmission was advanced for its time and consisted of a two-speed gearbox, the ratios being selected whilst the vehicle was stationary. The output shaft of the gearbox transmitted the power via spur gears and differential to the rear axle, the whole transmission being enclosed in an oil-tight casing. The brakes consisted of wooden blocks acting directly on the rear wheels, power operated by steam cylinders, and of course additional braking was available by selecting reverse. How you stopped the machine if you did not have steam up is uncertain. The use of Reid-Riekie spring spoke wheels helped to cushion the ride.

A Stewart-Thornycroft steam wagon for colonial use — The English Steam Wagon (© Trustees of the National Library of Scotland)

Thornycroft ceased the manufacture of steam wagons and concentrated on the manufacture of petrol engine-driven vehicles. From 1907 onwards the Thornycroft name was dropped and the wagon became the 'Stewart'. A new vertical boiler was adopted and several improvements were made. By 1909 the power had been raised from 45bhp to 50bhp and the valve gear consisted of a shaft, bevel driven from the centre of the crankshaft and lying parallel to the cylinders. The shaft carried cams which operated mushroom-type spring-returned valves similar to the Serpollet system, which is about as near to a poppet-valve overhead camshaft (OHC) arrangement as a steam engine can get. The gearbox, instead of employing sliding gears, was now of the epicyclic type, but the method of locking the drum and the internal gear carrier was by mechanical means; the gear ratio could then only be selected whilst stationary. The rear axle was driven by an enclosed worm gear of 16:1 ratio.

Manufacture was phased out in the later part of 1914 to make way for the production of munitions. However, a large number of vehicles had been made, many going overseas and to Crown Colonies where they acquired an excellent reputation for reliability. For a brief period Beardmore also owned Sentinel who manufactured steam wagons, acquired when he purchased the company of Alley and MacLellan in 1918. However, the wagon works near Shrewsbury was hived off as a separate company in which Beardmore had no financial interest.

Since William and his brother Joseph virtually owned the engineering works of Duncan Stewart Ltd, the steam wagon was Beardmore's first venture into mechanical road transport, just preceding his interest in Arrol-Johnston.

THE PAISLEY
ARROL-JOHNSTON

**The Paisley Arrol-Johnston – the three-cylinder desert vehicle –
the polar expedition – the first TT race**

SHORTLY after the establishment of the Stewart steam wagon, Beardmore
became involved with the manufacture of motorcars when Arrol-Johnston
moved their workshops to a factory in Paisley. The building had previously
been a cotton mill owned by the Coates family, who were also shareholders
in the Mo-Car Syndicate Ltd which financed the Arrol-Johnston car.
Beardmore joined the board of the newly-floated 'New Arrol-Johnston
Car Company Ltd' in 1902 and by 1905 had obtained complete financial
control. He achieved this by owning a majority of shares personally. This
investment was his own personal affair and Arrol-Johnston never became
part of the Beardmore industrial empire.

Mr Alistair Hacking crossing the line in the 1997 London to Brighton run
in his 12hp Arrol-Johnston Dogcart.

George Johnston of Arrol-Johnston was by training a locomotive engineer from the Hydepark Locomotive Company of Springburn, Glasgow. He had been commissioned by the Glasgow Corporation in 1894 to build a steam tramcar to replace the horse-drawn trams. (Unfortunately on the day of the final tests in front of the Corporation Committee, the tram caught fire and was totally destroyed.)

Johnston imported a Daimler in 1895, having owned a Panhard-Levassor previously. After extensive examination of the various continental makes of car, he became convinced that he could design a better machine and went to work on the project. By the end of the year the first British-built motor vehicle was ready for financial backing. Johnston was joined in the venture by Norman Osborne Fulton and T. Blackwood Murray. Fulton was in charge of manufacture and assembly; Blackwood Murray, an electrical engineer, set about designing an electrical system to replace the incandescent platinum tubes system. He also designed an electric vehicle with the intention of producing it in parallel with the petrol-engined car.

The petrol-engined car developed well. It had a top speed of 17 miles per hour (mph) and could climb a 1:5 gradient. Before the end of 1895 the Mo-Car Syndicate Ltd had been formed with Sir William Arrol as chairman, George Johnston as managing director, Fulton as works manager and Blackwood Murray as commercial manager. The product was the Arrol-Johnston car and the factory was at Camlachie. The company was registered in 1899 as a joint stock company with a capital of £50,000. Its main product was a six-seater dog-cart with a two-cylinder engine employing four opposed pistons and a system of rocking levers connecting the crankshaft.

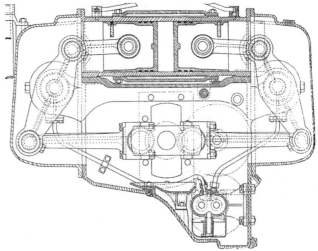

1905 Arrol-Johnston engine — section, showing two of the pistons with their connecting rods, etc. Adjacent to the cylinder shown and in the same casting is another similar cylinder with the two pistons operating rocking levers which transmitted reciprocating motion via connecting rods to the crankshaft.
(Courtesy of Mitchell Library)

Capacity was three litres, rated at 12hp. The company also produced a three-cylinder 16hp or 20hp Tonneau (described more fully on page 16).

A four-speed gearbox was driven via a chain from the engine, and a further chain from the gearbox drove the rear axle. The brakes consisted of shoes or spoons pressed against the rubber-tyred wheels. The steering wheel and controls were situated in the centre, behind the front seats, and the engine was started by pulling on a rope wound around a drum. Once underway the vehicle was said to be quiet and vibrationless.

As a result of a disastrous fire the company was forced to move to new premises in Paisley where production recommenced in 1902. Before this, however, Blackwood Murray and Fulton had left the company in order to start the Albion Motor Car Company Ltd in 1899.

The Arrol-Johnston company was restructured financially in 1903. New finance, mainly from Beardmore, became available and there were important changes in staff. George Johnston left as a result of a disagreement and started up the All British Car Company, a venture that was to be short-lived.

Arrol-Johnston under this new management was revitalised. J. S. Napier, no relation to the London car firm, had been managing director since 1902 and he now took over the responsibilities of chief engineer in 1904/5. He produced a horizontal twin-cylinder car 121 x 165mm, 3.8 litre, the design being similar to the dog-cart engine of 1899. Napier was keenly interested

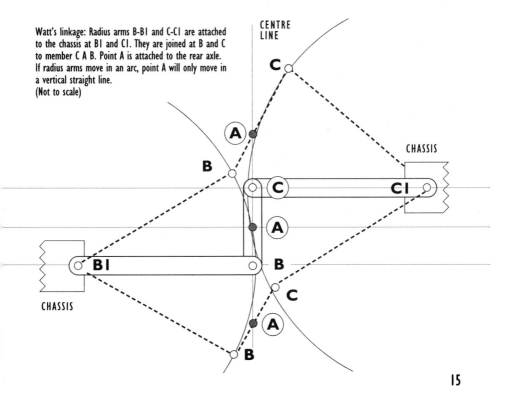

Watt's linkage: Radius arms B-BI and C-CI are attached to the chassis at BI and CI. They are joined at B and C to member C A B. Point A is attached to the rear axle. If radius arms move in an arc, point A will only move in a vertical straight line. (Not to scale)

in motor racing and he appears to have had the enthusiastic backing of the new chairman. Meanwhile the association with the Mo-Car Syndicate appears to have ceased in 1905, as did the Coates family investment.

These cars, with the exception of the engine, were very modern in design and a complete break away from the earlier dog-cart. Suspension was by half elliptics at the front and three-quarter elliptics at the rear. The engine was mounted well back in the chassis, and that and the four-speed gearbox amidships must have brought the centre of gravity to almost mid-point. Drive from the gearbox to the rear axle was by open propeller shaft with sliding trunnion universal joints at each end. The rear universal incorporated an internal expanding brake and an unusual spring drive which, it was claimed, ironed out all irregularities. Great care was taken to locate the rear axle positively; radius rods attached to each side of the frame took care of torque and lozenging forces, whilst a Watt's linkage (see page 15) across the frame and attached to the rear axle housing ensured only straight up and down movement. The steering gear, which was adjustable for rake, was of the worm and nut type.

The engine was increased to $4^3/4$ inch bore x $6^1/2$ inch stroke. The normal speed was 800 rev/min; controlled by a 'hit and miss' governor on the exhaust the maximum rev/min was 1100. Inlet valves were automatic air suction type and ignition was by low-tension magneto. At 800 rev/min, speeds were first gear 9.4mph, second 21.8mph, third 31.6mph, and fourth 45mph. Rudge wire spoke wheels were used.

Two of these cars were entered for the 1905 Tourist Trophy (TT) under the name of Arrol-Johnston. The cars were successful, J. S. Napier driving his car into first place and Percy Northey, with the second car, managing fourth.

The cars were offered to the public in detuned form. However, in spite of the advanced design, four-speed gearboxes and Hele Shaw clutch (a great advance over the then popular leather-faced cone clutch), they encountered some sales resistance due to the opposed piston, horizontal twin-cylinder engine which, it must be admitted, was not entirely satisfactory. The winning of the 1905 TT was regarded as a lucky shot. A smaller and less sporting 12hp version was also produced, but it was less successful.

In 1903 a 20hp three-cylinder car had been brought out. It had the unusual feature of different-sized cylinder bores, the central cylinder being larger than the two outer ones, giving a capacity of over four litres. The arrangement was claimed to provide excellent balance. The engine was installed sloping forwards and transversely in the frame, thus pre-empting Alec Issigonis, Austin's brilliant chief engineer, and his popular cross-mounted engine 'MINI' by several years.

The transmission was by chain to the gearbox and thence by chain to the rear axle, and was greatly simplified by this arrangement. The three-cylinder car did not stay in production for much more than a year, but it formed the basis of the first 'off road' vehicle to be produced in Britain, if not the world. The three-cylinder chassis with its large diameter wheels, high ground clearance, short wheel base and relatively wide track, made it very suitable for use on rough terrain.

The vehicle was built to the order of the Egyptian government and the Sirdar, Major General Sir Francis Reginald Wingate KCMG (father of General Orde Wingate of 'Chindits' fame). In order to cope with the uncertainties of the fuel supplies in Egypt the engine was fitted with two carburettors, one of which operated on petrol and the other on paraffin. A rotary valve in the induction manifold selected whichever carburettor was required. The vehicle was designed to operate under conditions of extreme heat, dust and loose sand, not to mention rocky outcrops. The engine compartment was completely sealed against the ingress of sand and the transmission chains were totally encased. Great care was taken to exclude sand from all moving parts by means of an apron which sealed the underside of the chassis. A winch ensured that the vehicle could pull itself out of soft areas and also climb steep slopes. The tyres were solid rubber with a flat profile 3½ inches wide, experiments having shown this to have provided the optimum surface area to avoid sinking in soft ground and also to avoid the building up of a ridge in front of the wheels.

The wheels were fully enclosed between light gauge steel discs in order to prevent sand from being thrown up by the spokes, and provision was made so that paddles could be attached to the rims to increase traction in soft ground. A draw-bar was fitted at the rear for the purpose of towing a two-wheeled trailer equipped with a 'Mavor & Coulson' searchlight and generator, the latter being driven via the power take-off, which consisted of a shaft and pulley projecting from the gearbox at the side of the vehicle and driving the generator by means of a flat belt. Naturally the provision of an adequate water supply for the engine and the crew (which could be as many as seven) was very important, and tanks were fitted beneath the seats within the body-work. A range of 200 miles was possible on one tank of fuel and sufficient provisions were carried to last for three days. Maximum speed was 20mph; very good considering that the vehicle weighed two tons four hundred-weight and the trailer just over one ton. There are no reports of the vehicle's performance, but it must have been reasonably successful as a further order was placed in 1908 for a more conventional design that incorporated the lessons learned and some of the features of the three-cylinder car.

If this first vehicle could be regarded as a forerunner to the Land Rover, the second vehicle was the precursor of the Range Rover and was based on Napier's latest design, the 38/45hp with four-cylinder engine, overhead inlet valves and side exhaust. The nominal rating was 45hp, but a maximum of 75hp was available. As on the first vehicle, elaborate precautions were taken to exclude sand from the working parts. A report in the *Automotive Journal* of 1908 states that the wheel rims were of cast steel and the heavy gauge steel discs were load bearers. These assemblies, complete with wide-profile solid rubber tyres, must have been extremely heavy and contributed to a very uncomfortable ride. As before, paddles could be attached to the rims to assist traction.

The body was of considerable interest. It was designed to seat seven with the driver and one other in front; the rear portion, which looked very much like a normal touring car, was fitted with two rows of seats crosswise. The first row seated two persons, with a passageway in between, and the rear row seated three. The body panels were carried on a light gauge steel frame so arranged that if a panel was damaged it could easily be removed and replaced, a system later employed on the Land Rover. An additional steel frame carried a roof fitted with retaining rails so that extra equipment could be stacked. The transmission was conventional and followed standard Arrol-Johnston practice, except that the gearbox and rear axle were strengthened to cope with the increased loads that the heavy wheels and generally rough conditions were likely to impose. Suspension was by half elliptics in front and double elliptics at the rear, and the system must have had its work cut out for it to cope.

A maximum speed of 35mph was quoted with the cautious comment that the average speed would be about 18mph. Nonetheless these two desert cars represented a great deal of original and far-sighted thought and a surprising understanding of the conditions likely to be encountered.

In 1909 yet another 'off road' vehicle appeared in the guise of the Antarctic exploration cars designed for the then Lieutenant Ernest Shackleton RN expedition to the South Pole. This car must have been designed concurrently with the desert cars and more diverse conditions can hardly be imagined, although at least one of the problems was the same, namely that of traction over soft surfaces.

The vehicle Arrol-Johnston used had a four-cylinder air-cooled engine of 12-15hp with push-rod operated overhead inlet valves and side exhaust. The chassis was similar to a previous design, having half elliptics in front and three-quarter elliptics at the rear. The body consisted of two seats open-sided, with a 'pick-up'-type rear capable of carrying a load of 18cwt.

Reports in the technical press at the time are misleading as many confused the engine with designs produced by Arrol-Johnston; in fact it was a Simms unit with Simms-Bosch magneto. The engine compartment was completely sealed, no fan was fitted and it relied on the surrounding low temperature for cooling. In addition to the magneto, coil ignition was also provided, but as the electrolyte in the accumulators froze solid this system was of no use.

The exhaust gasses provided several useful functions: one to heat a foot warmer and another to melt snow to provide drinking water. More importantly, the carburettor was surrounded by a jacket of hot gasses to aid vaporisation; and a further jacket surrounded a can of oil since topping up the sump was found to be a slow and difficult process, despite the fact that non-freezing oil had been supplied by Prices Patent Candle Company. Also, sight drip-feed lubricators had to be placed inside the engine compartment because external pipes tended to freeze.

A variety of wheels was taken along with the expedition. One set was shod with wood to overcome freeze welding of metal to ice, the rear wheels being provided with steel (alternatively wooden) spuds, whilst a set of skis could be attached to the front wheels. Dunlop also supplied rubber tyres to which Parsons chains could be attached.

In practice the car could pull two sledges carrying 1500lbs and three people at 8mph in second gear on flat sea ice, but the speed dropped to 5mph on snow. According to Shackleton the vehicle was only marginally successful, but this was more likely because no one understood the best way to use mechanical transport under Arctic or any other conditions. Nevertheless, Arrol-Johnston gained much favourable publicity and, of course, valuable experience. They were the pioneers, but their experience was not put to use until many years later.

The South Polar Arrol-Johnston Car for the 1907-9 Shackleton Expedition. (National Motor Museum)
The rear wheels shod with iron are used to grip the snow; and spikes added when surfaces are hard or slippery.

The fact that a new mode of transport over frozen wastelands and soft ground had been developed seems to have escaped attention. Despite being a successful design, it was a new concept and its potential was not well enough understood. Ironically, had this vehicle been subjected to logical development, vast areas of frozen land in Northern Europe and Canada might have been opened up years before they were eventually explored. Or, further ahead, it might have become the forerunner of the tank or anticipated the Citroën Kegresse, the car which had four rear wheels which carried tracks similar to those of a tank. This lack of vision was uncharacteristic of Beardmore, but 1909 was the year that Thomas Charles Willis Pullinger became general manager and it is unlikely that anything so unorthodox and imaginative would have figured in his plans for the future. It was left to others to make the idea a practicality. (Incidentally, the Beardmore 'Glacier' was named by Shackleton after his sponsor.)

During Napier's period the company launched out into commercial vehicle manufacture. Originally using the opposed piston engines, they offered 10cwt and 15cwt vans and a bus chassis but never managed to make much impression in the market. An example of the two-ton bus chassis was exhibited at Liverpool in 1907 and the Woolton Motor Bus Company purchased two of them; while a lorry in the service of Messrs Waring and Gillow was said to be giving both trouble-free and economical service. The transmission was similar to the car, employing the four-speed gearbox and spring drive universal joint. A bevel-driven counter shaft with differential was mounted ahead of the rear axle and the drive was transmitted by chains enclosed in an oil-tight chain case. The works manager at this time was Ernest A. Rosenheim, who was to be responsible for the preparation of the 1908 TT cars.

Arrol-Johnston was back again for the 1906 TT, but tyre troubles apart it was apparent that the cars were no match for the opposition. The winning vehicle was a Rolls-Royce that recorded a winning speed of 39.8mph, more than double the speed of the Arrol-Johnston in 1905. Arrol-Johnston continued in competition without much success and by 1907 they were in financial difficulties. Nevertheless, in what was to become a typical reaction to adversity on the part of Beardmore, they entered the 1908 TT with a team of very rakish-looking cars which used four-cylinder engines based on Napier's new inlet over exhaust (IOE) design. This was the 'four inch' race so the bores were reduced to meet the race regulations, ie 102mm, giving a capacity of 4.1 litres. These cars could attain speeds of 80mph and the drivers were Dario Resta, G. C. G. Moss and E. J. Cyril Roberts. The team, alas, was out of luck, although their performance was a considerable improvement on their 1906 efforts. An accident to one car and shortage of fuel on the last lap of another eliminated the team. However, Roberts on the third car was among the leaders for the first six laps.

In 1907 Arrol-Johnston was producing about 700 cars per year, the range consisting of two large four-cylinder models (24/30 and 38/45), as well as the 12/15 twin-cylinder car. The cars had many technical innovations and were well to the front among the leaders in the large-car market.

In 1908 the 24/30 was replaced with a Napier-designed 16/25 with overhead inlet valves and side-valve exhaust which, as mentioned, formed the basis of that year's TT team. The financial affairs of the company had also improved, if only marginally.

John S. Napier, backed by Beardmore, had put Arrol-Johnston among the leaders in technical innovation. Unfortunately, Napier was unable to achieve the same success financially. At the end of 1908 he left the company, eventually reappearing at the Cubitt Car Company at Aylesbury. One cannot help feeling that, despite his apparent lack of business acumen, Arrol-Johnston was never quite the same after Napier's departure.

Radiator view of the 1906 4-litre Arrol-Johnston TT car. (Glasgow Museums and Art Galleries)

Arrol-Johnston Dogcart 1901. (Glasgow Museums and Art Galleries)

21

THE DUMFRIES ARROL-JOHNSTON,
THE GALLOWAY
AND THE PULLINGER ERA

The Pullinger era – Theo Biggs – the 15.9 car

*'One of the greatest pains to human nature
is the pain of a new idea.'*
WALTER BAGEHOT 1826-77

IN 1909 a significant event took place. Thomas Charles Willis Pullinger took over as general manager, bringing with him Darracq, Sunbeam and Humber experience – and also his daughter, Dorothée (of whom more later). He also brought along Theodore James Biggs, designer of the 1908 Beeston Humber TT cars, and J. Reid who had driven one of those cars in the race. Another helper was Willie Lowe, in charge of sales and destined to take over from Pullinger later on.

Pullinger was a highly-intelligent man with a record of successful management and an intimate knowledge of motorcar manufacture on both sides of the Channel. Educated at Dartford Grammar School, he was also a qualified and experienced engineer, having served a seven-year apprenticeship with Messrs J. & L. Hall of Dartford. He then worked as a draughtsman at Woolwich Arsenal where he became interested in bicycles, before moving to Harris and Carter who invented the oil-bath chain case.

1908 Humber Beeston engine.
(Demaus Transport Photographics)

Pullinger started his own business as a bicycle manufacturer but after two years sold out and joined Humber who despatched him to Paris to supervise arrangements for a factory that was to be built in the French capital. But the project fell through and in 1892 he joined Darracq, who were at that time only cycle manufacturers. As works manager

Pullinger organised the production of the successful 'Gladiator' motor-cycle, and his efficient methods enabled the company to be very competitive.

Pullinger's only contact with Darracq after they had moved into car manufacture was to supervise the production of three eleven-litre 'British' Darracqs at the Glasgow factory of G. & J. Weir. This venture was destined to be unsuccessful, however, as the cars were not completed in time for the 1904 Gordon Bennett race.

During his time with Darracq Pullinger married a French girl. In 1894 he became works manager for Duncan & Superbe who manufactured the D. S. motorcycle, a copy of the Hildebrand & Wolfmüller machine. Here he claimed to have played a part in the design and manufacture of a small car with a two-cylinder horizontally-opposed engine, driven through a two-speed gearbox operated by friction clutches. The vehicle employed a tubular frame and accommodated two seats side by side.

In 1896 he was running a tube mill at Lyon-Vaise (Rhone) and later joined Teste & Monet where again he was involved in the design and manufacture of 'La Mouche', a 2¼hp water-cooled cylinder head, single-cylinder car with either two or four seats. However, there is no independent confirmation of his claim to have designed these machines. A year later he was responsible for the production of a 14hp car which was entered for the Coupe de Sud Est. Unfortunately the car crashed in practice, so Pullinger entered the 6hp car which he drove himself, winning his class.

Upon his return to England Pullinger joined Sunbeam where his managerial expertise enabled him to turn the loss-making company into profitability in one year. In his retirement speech in 1926 he claimed to have designed the chain-driven 12hp Sunbeam car which also employed Harris and Carter oil-bath chain cases, but in actual fact it was a direct copy of the 12hp Berliet. With Louis Coatalen as engineering director and B. J. Angus-

1912 '15.9' car. Engine of 15.9 offside; and nearside.
(Photographs courtesy of the late Brian Porter)

Shaw as chief engineer, one may well ask what the works manager was doing in the drawing office anyway.

Pullinger moved from Sunbeam to become works manager at Humber's Beeston factory. When that factory closed he became works manager of the Coventry factory, remaining there until 1909 when he became general manager of Arrol-Johnston and managing director a year later. Due to Pullinger's undoubted managerial talents, and assisted by Theo Bigg's excellent design, Arrol-Johnston expanded, outgrowing the Paisley factory and resulting in a move to Dumfries, a move which Pullinger planned and masterminded.

In 1912-13 Pullinger visited the Ford factory in America and it is said that the Dumfries factory at Heathhall was a copy of the Ford Highlands factory in the United States.

Pullinger was a man of enormous drive and energy, exercising a dominant 'hands-on' approach over the entire company. As happens so often under such management the more independent members of staff tended to seek alternative employment where their talents were better appreciated.

He was also an old friend of William Morris, having met when they were both members of the Catford Cycle Club. Morris was keen to join forces with Pullinger, but given the latter's dogmatic views on motorcar production it is not surprising that he disagreed with Morris' approach to car manufacture.

It was Pullinger's weakness that he seemed unable to grasp any new concept in conflict with his own preconceived ideas. One of his first acts at Arrol-Johnston, for example, was to scrap all Napier's designs, including development work on the 'off road' vehicles. Less than four years later, as the British Army struggled in the mud of Flanders, they were denied experience and expertise that could have led to the earlier development of the tank or some other form of armoured vehicle capable of traversing soft ground.

[In 1912 E. H. Mole of Adelaide, Australia submitted plans for a tracked vehicle to the War Office. They were rejected and he resubmitted his plans in 1914. In 1916, against considerable opposition, a tracked vehicle was eventually developed, so perhaps Napier's designs would have suffered the same fate at the hands of the short-sighted War Office.]

Theo Biggs stayed long enough to play the major part in the design of the new 15.9 four-cylinder SV Arrol-Johnston which adopted the rear-mounted radiator, a feature of the TT Beeston Humber. Another feature of Biggs' design was the use of double elliptics on the rear suspension. This of course employed the radius rods and Watt's linkage of the previous Napier-designed cars, the Watt's linkage being re-named the Arrol-Johnston anti-roll linkage (see diagram on page 15). He also retained the ring and stud universal joints.

Biggs returned to Humber (Coventry) on 15 April 1912, having been with Arrol-Johnston for three years almost to the day. He left Humber for the second time in November 1914 to join his old friend Frank E. Baker,

1912 15.9 Arrol-Johnston.
(Photograph courtesy of Richard Daggert)

and will reappear in this book when the Humber connection crops up again.

The Theo Biggs 15.9 was the first new design to appear under the new management. It was a conventional side-valve four-cylinder with cylinder blocks cast in pairs, and non-detachable cylinder heads. It was one of the first examples of unit construction; the bottom half of the crankcase and gearbox formed an aluminium bedplate, making a neat and very strong structure (see page 31). A 'coal scuttle' bonnet discretely enclosed the 'works'. A four-speed gearbox was fitted and, in its original form, four wheel brakes of Allan Liversige pattern. Like all innovations some development was required before the system could be made to work satisfactorily. But Pullinger was reluctant. In his view, front wheel brakes, like shock absorbers, were not really necessary and the model reverted to rear wheel brakes only.

A smaller model rated at 11.9hp, and later a 23.8hp SV six-cylinder model, were also on offer. In 1911 one of the 11.9 cars lapped Brooklands at a very respectable 56mph. However, despite the advent of Pullinger and his apparently strongly-professed beliefs that racing improved the breed, not to mention an experienced design team in support, Arrol-Johnston's sporting successes were few and their activities declined in that area.

In 1911 three 15.9hp cars were entered in the Coupe des Voiturettes Légeres at Boulogne, but the best they could achieve was seventh place. However, they proved to be reliable, winning the team prize – all three cars were still running at the end of the race.

Just prior to joining Arrol-Johnston, Biggs was working on the design of a revolutionary all-aluminium engine, overhead camshaft (OHC) operating three valves per cylinder, two exhaust and one inlet valve. Presumably it is this engine which, according to rumour, was intended for the 1912 TT cars.

However, it never appeared in public. The engine may not have made its race debut, but it undoubtedly existed. Its absence from the 1912 events could have been due to Pullinger's conservative model policy, and might also have been the reason for Theo Biggs' departure. But Pullinger's rather unexciting approach to design development was in this case supported by valid financial reasons; his main responsibility was to ensure the continued profitability of the company. He had formulated a policy which was to produce reliable, good quality (if somewhat mundane) transport aimed at the upper middle-class family man. Biggs' all-aluminium OHC engine was expensive to make, and if a commercial version were to be produced it would only appeal to a very small sector of the public. Pullinger was a strong advocate of a single model policy. This made sound financial sense, provided that the single model was sufficiently attractive to the public. Pullinger thought the 15.9 car would fulfil that role and a top of the market sports car could not be considered. This situation was soon to be overtaken by developments within Beardmores, connected with Dr Ing Ferdinand Porsche, which dominated the scene until 1918.

Biggs' departure in April 1912 left Arrol-Johnston without the services of a design engineer. This deficiency was not made good until 1916 with the arrival of another ex-Humber engineer, G. W. A. Brown, who had designed the 1908 TT OHC Coventry Humber car. Brown had had a distinguished career, having designed the Austin Pearly racers and then the Clement-Talbot 25/50, the first car to exceed 100mph at Brooklands, driven by Percy Lambert. Brown subsequently designed the 10.4 Coventry Premier. It should also be noted that Brown was a Beardmore employee attached to the Dalmuir engine works and therefore not under Pullinger's all-encompassing control.

With no OHC engines available for the 1912 competition season, the 15.9 SV engine was modified by increasing the stroke to 140mm for use in the 1912 Coupe de l'Auto race at Dieppe. These cars were finished in tartan paint of the Gordon clan (green and blue). They had five-speed gearboxes giving an overdrive top with a theoretical speed of 117mph, although it is doubtful if the engines developed sufficient torque at 3000 rev/min to achieve that speed; the cars sounded more suitable for a speed record attempt at Brooklands rather than a road race in France. In fact the best they could do was to finish fifth. Interestingly, two of the cars had chain drive to the rear axle, presumably for ease of changing the axle ratio; the other cars had normal live axles with bevel drive, and these were fitted with friction shock absorbers on the rear axle. After 1912 and the departure of Biggs, despite the enthusiasm of Beardmore, there was a growing dissent, mainly from Pullinger, about the direction the company was taking. It is also difficult to see how Pullinger could reconcile his extremely conservative views with the essentially innovative thinking required in the design of a successful competition car.

In view of the post-war cars produced by Pullinger, after the 'Victory' debacle (see page 28) it seems as if he had lost whatever enthusiasm he might have had. Arrol-Johnston never raced again until after the retirement of Pullinger, and then only as Arrol-Aster.

In the meantime the development of the new Austro Daimler Porsche aero engine was taking centre stage, and except for annual refinements the 1909 range of models lasted until 1913 when the six-cylinder 23.8hp car was dropped.

In 1913 Arrol-Johnston became a public company and the word 'new' was dropped from the title. The money raised by this flotation was used to finance the new factory at Heathhall. According to Michael Moss, in his book *Beardmore, The History of a Scottish Industrial Giant,* it was also used to purchase a shareholding in the Aster Engineering Company (1913) Ltd, Aster having just completed a financial reorganisation. Unfortunately the financial records of both companies are incomplete, so while no confirmation of the deal can be found it is a fact that Beardmore and Aster co-operated with each other long before the amalgamation with Arrol-Johnston in 1927, and a 1913 deal makes a lot of sense. It may have been an agreement to purchase technology rather than the purchase of shares. In 1913 Aster were manufacturing the six-cylinder Green aero engine which had won the British government prize in 1909 for the best British aero engine. Aster probably had more experience in aero engine manufacture than any other company. They had an excellent reputation for high-class workmanship and their experience and know-how would obviously have been of the greatest value to Arrol-Johnston in the production of Beardmore aero engines.

Details of the Arrol-Johnston flotation, dated 7 May 1913, are as follows. The directors were William Beardmore of Parkhead Forge, Glasgow; Thomas Charles Willis Pullinger of Swinlees, Ayrshire; and David Sturrock of Carntyne Iron Works, Parkhead. The new flotation was £80,000, six per cent redeemable debenture stock. The company had a nominal capital of £100,000, consisting of £1 ordinary shares. Beardmore owned 24,419, Pullinger 9975 and Sturrock 500. Five thousand shares were transferred to William Carnegie and James Reid of the National Bank of Scotland.

David Sturrock died in 1915 and his shares were transferred to Major Herbert Rowan Alexander of Troqueer, Dumfries. Beardmore took over 5000 shares lodged with the National Bank, thus increasing his holding to 29,419, making him by far the largest shareholder.

★   ★   ★

As the war in France turned in favour of the Allies, there was a rush to prepare new models to greet the new world. Arrol-Johnston's pre-war models were basically 1909 designs, so they started work with a clean sheet of paper on a model called 'Victory'. Since Arrol-Johnston did not officially have a chief designer (automobiles), G. W. A. Brown was entrusted with the design. The new car was to incorporate the latest engineering techniques, including automatic chassis lubrication, and was to have sporting potential. Due to the circumstances of the war and impending peace, the car had to be designed and tested as quickly as possible. Whilst there is no doubt that Brown had all his technical notes and drawings of the 1908 Coventry Humber, Arrol-Johnston already had working drawings of a four-cylinder OHC engine based on the Beeston Humber and, in addition, the Dalmuir works had already built a small light-weight engine to Brown's design to meet a War Office specification. This engine was a four-cylinder OHC with the camshaft operating inclined valves driven by skew gears. The capacity was 1487cc. The mechanical layout and the use of skew gears and inclined valves sound very similar to the Beeston Humber.

Technical information concerning the 'Victory' engine is hard to find, but its mechanical specification was also the same as the small Beardmore engine, the only difference being a three-bearing crankshaft and the bore/stroke ratio. The 'Victory' engine was four-cylinders 2.6 litres, but by the time the car reached the distributors the capacity was 2.8 litres. There was talk of a larger engine, presumably 3.5 litres, but there is no evidence that it ever got any further than the discussion phase.

The 'Victory' in 2.6 litre form was announced by Arrol-Johnston in 1918 and many original features were incorporated, including some which were highly undesirable, such as a transmission brake. Due to production delays, which seem to have included extensive engine redesign, the car did not reach the dealers until August 1919. The 'Victory' should have been the car of the year and did indeed create great interest, but an unfortunate series of events turned it into a complete fiasco and it was hastily withdrawn.

Undoubtedly the 'Victory' was very much Beardmore's personal project. It was designed at the Dalmuir Works by Brown, thus tightening Beardmore's control over Arrol-Johnston. The company's aero engine experience was

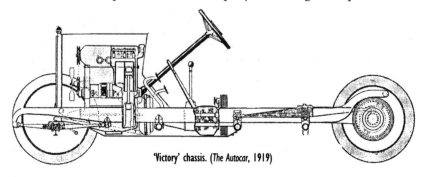

'Victory' chassis. (*The Autocar*, 1919)

emphasised and the whole design was claimed to be light with a very good power to weight ratio. According to Captain E. M. Wright, ex-Royal Flying Corps (RFC), motoring correspondent for a London daily paper and syndicated press, the 'Victory' in sports car form could have given the new Bentley cars some strong competition. Considering that the smaller Beardmore car in 2.0 litre form and with a two-bearing crankshaft was to beat the Bugatti of Raymond Mays and the Vauxhall of Humphrey Cook, and break the record at Shelsley Walsh in 1924, there are strong grounds for believing that the 2.8 litre engine in a lighter and less expensive chassis than the Bentley could have been developed into a very formidable car.

The impression gained over the years is that the 'Victory' was a revolutionary design and insufficiently tested before being offered to the public. It is alleged to have suffered a variety of mechanical failures which were too deep-seated to be rectified, and that the only course of action was to withdraw the car. However, this is entirely incorrect. The 'Victory' design was by no means revolutionary, and in the main it consisted of tried and tested components incorporated in a thoroughly up-to-date concept. The chassis had the same track as the 1914 15.9 car and the wheel base was only three inches shorter. Half elliptic springs in front with cantilever rear suspension made for a simple and uncomplicated layout. The rear axle was positively located by means of a torque tube which was anchored just behind the gearbox.

The original announcement gave the bore and stroke as 75mm x 150mm and this caused some comment in the technical press, such a long stroke in relation to the bore being unusual even in those days. However, when the car eventually became available, the bore and stroke were 80mm x 140mm. This change brought the 'Victory' in line with the Arrol-Johnston Coupe de l'Auto cars of the 1912 and 1913 versions of the 15.9. It is likely that Brown based much of his design on Biggs' work since he was very familiar with it, having copied the 15.9 Arrol-Johnston engine extensively in the design of the Beardmore taxi engine (see page 57).

Thus the 'Victory' was exciting and technically very advanced, with a tremendous potential for development. Not surprisingly the company was swamped with orders when the car was displayed at the 1919 motor show. The truth concerning the mechanical shortcomings of the 'Victory' is more bizarre than any speculation about faulty design. It was plain and simple sabotage, according to the version of events given by Beardmore's nephew, W. J. M. Beardmore. It appeared that the company provided a car for use by the Prince of Wales during his tour of the West Country. The 'Victory' was quite a fast car and the driver, for some unknown reason and without authorisation, took the car out on his own, probably to see how it would perform. Going too fast he lost control, the car skidded and ended up in a ditch. To cover himself the driver declared that the brakes had failed, the steering was faulty, and the car was dangerous – which was untrue. The car had not broken down.

According to Michael Pullinger, son of Thomas, another version of this story states that the driver was disgruntled because the company had omitted to give him a 'back-hander' and the ditching of the car was deliberate. The press reported the facts inaccurately and, as is usually the case where royalty is involved, greatly exaggerated everything. The upshot was that the Prince abandoned the tour because the car was a write-off, inferred as mechanical failure. This was a cover-up by the Prince's staff. The explanation, which was a pack of lies, was accepted without anybody then or later seeking the truth. The days of investigative journalism had not yet arrived.

If Pullinger had been looking for an excuse, then the debacle of the Prince of Wales' tour could not have happened at a more opportune moment. He seized the opportunity to exert his authority and halt production of the 'Victory'. Not only did he consider its design to be unorthodox, but he also resented Brown who was not under his control. He was determined that no more designs would be foisted upon him from outside.

In the battle for overall power Beardmore was beginning to find himself no match for Pullinger who out-manoeuvred him. In one stroke the latter swept away all external influences and established himself as the only authority and controller of Arrol-Johnston. This left Beardmore still chairman and major shareholder, but with virtually no role to play.

However, by ceasing production on the 'Victory', Pullinger effectively blocked the services of Brown, a talented design engineer, at a time when he had no comparable designer to replace him. The car, an outstanding development with an exciting potential and an overflowing waiting list of customers, was sabotaged. In exchange for this, Pullinger offered a design which was twelve years old and in urgent need of modernisation.

Beardmore accepted this state of affairs largely because of his own inade-quacy as an administrator. The cessation of aero engine manufacture need not have been a setback, but attempts to re-establish it at Coatbridge were to prove expensive and unsuccessful. According to W. J. M. Beardmore, Pullinger was now too strongly entrenched to be overruled. Arrol-Johnston had enjoyed a period of prosperity since Pullinger became works manager, a situation not experienced under Napier or Rosenheim. Beardmore was left with no choice but to hand over control to Pullinger, whose past successes seemed to promise continued prosperity for the future. It was only when Pullinger assumed the roll of policymaker that the cracks began to show.

No one should underestimate Pullinger's forceful character and tough-ness, and his obsessive determination to brook no interference or criticism. However, the 'Victory' was arguably the most important car ever built by Arrol-Johnston. Had the design been developed it would have changed the character of the company irrevocably. Instead its demise set the pattern for the company's future development, or lack of such. From 1922 onwards the fortunes of Arrol-Johnston declined, the design office virtually ceased to exist since nothing new was required of it, and the whole organisation, lacking a stimulus, lost its enthusiasm – mostly due to the inflexible nature of Thomas Pullinger.

The 'Victory' car design was sold to the Phoenix Company of Letchworth. Brown joined them as chief engineer, but the company lacked sufficient capital to develop and market the car and the true potential of the design was never realised.

Beardmore remained chairman of Arrol-Johnston, but diverted his energies into producing a range of cars under his own name. Having won the battle, Pullinger revived the 15.9 car with a frontal radiator and new bodywork to cover the outdated engine and chassis, using as many 'Victory' parts as could be salvaged. The 'new' car was offered to the public as 'of known design and materials' and assurance given that it contained no untried innovations. Indeed, what else could be said about a twelve year-old design?

A last attempt was made to produce a car of more modern aspect than the revived 15.9. The company ordered 50 OHV (overhead valves) six-cylinder Hotchkiss engines. It is not known how many, if any, of these engines were delivered, and nothing further transpired. This was probably due to the fact that William Morris decided that his newly-acquired Hotchkiss engine factory would henceforth concentrate on supplying engines for Morris cars alone, to the exclusion of outside customers.

This retreat from progress had, however, at least one positive aspect. At £625 the 15.9 was one of the cheapest and best-equipped cars of its size in a car-hungry market. Its engine was not modernised until 1921 and then the redesign was far less comprehensive than Brown's taxi engine (see page 56). The updating consisted mainly of a monoblock cylinder casting and detachable head. The unit construction was the same as Theo Biggs' original

1922 15.9hp base plate-type unit construction Arrol-Johnston.
(Photograph courtesy of Mitchell Library)

design and consisted of an aluminium base frame that included the oil sump of the engine, a fly wheel and clutch pit and the sump of the gearbox, with a flexible coupling connecting the clutch shaft to the gearbox. (Pullinger could have had Brown's much more up-to-date version just for the asking.) The rear double elliptic springs, radius rods and Watt's linkage were retained, but were subject to criticism in the motoring press. Nevertheless Arrol-Johnston was among the leaders in volume production of cars. It employed about 1600 men and output reached 50 cars per week, thus vindicating Pullinger's policies and management methods – but only in the short term.

Some years after the 'Victory' debacle, my father was talked into buying a 1922 15.9 open tourer. The car was secondhand but in immaculate condition, having been owned by one of the company directors. It had many extra fittings, one of which was an 'Auster' auxiliary windscreen of massive proportions to shield the passengers in the rear seat from the elements. It was a heavy affair with side screens and complicated articulated arms which enabled it to be stowed away behind the front seat without sacrificing leg room. The main disadvantage was that the serrated locking devices, which held it in position, invariably worked loose, causing the screen to fall backwards and strike the unfortunate passengers on the head. If the 'Victory' had a high power to weight ratio, the 15.9 Arrol-Johnston was the extreme opposite. It was, to say the least, solid and took about a mile of straight road to achieve 45mph.

★   ★   ★

Arrol-Johnston continued to build solid, over-engineered and uninteresting cars. The 15.9 car for the 1922 season had an increased stroke to 130mm, raising the horsepower to 36 at 2000 rev/min. More importantly, the rear suspension was now half elliptics, and the rear axle was located at the rear of the gearbox by means of a torque tube anchored in phosphor bronze bushes. Since the wheel base had been increased to ten feet, the same as the 'Victory', it is very likely that the torque tube and rear axle were also identical, thus conveniently using up 'Victory' parts. In 1923 the dynamo drive from the rear of the camshaft was discontinued and this unit and the magneto were driven in tandem from a silent chain in the timing case at the front.

The single-model policy had to be abandoned. The 15.9 car did not generate sufficient sales and a 3.5 litre 'Empire' model, designed to capture the colonial market, was produced in 1924. It did not, however, capture that market. Also introduced in the same year was a 2.1 litre 'fourteen'. The colonial model had neither front wheel brakes nor shock absorbers. In 1925 the 'fourteen' was replaced by a 'twelve', the 15.9 continued with the 130mm stroke, and the Empire tourer continued, still without front wheel brakes. A Galloway which shared the same engine as the 'twelve' was also in production. In 1926 Pullinger was persuaded to go on a world tour prior to his retirement. While he was away other forces went to work.

Side valves now gave way to overhead push-rod operated valves, and there is reason to suspect that these engines were designed by Aster Engineering Company especially for Arrol-Johnston. The Arrol-Johnston sales literature of the time went to great lengths to explain the reasons for the change, stressing higher efficiency and better accessibility as well as quieter operation. Rolls-Royce was quoted as proof that push-rod operation was the best method. Another long-overdue change was the adoption of a bell housing to enclose the clutch and join the gearbox in unit construction. The old aluminium casting incorporating the engine sump, clutch and flywheel pit and gearbox sump was expensive to produce and conferred no advantage, and only Pullinger's resistance to change had kept it in service for so long. Having made this sweeping change, the company had nothing new to offer in 1927 and was in the process of becoming Arrol-Aster.

To keep the staff employed the company undertook the reconstruction of Sir Malcolm Campbell's 'Bluebird' for his attempt on the landspeed record at Daytona. Beardmore's association with landspeed record breakers is interesting. In 1926 Captain Irving, designer of Major Segrave's 'Golden Arrow' and Campbell's 'Bluebird', was called in as consultant to the ailing Beardmore Motor Company which was facing financial trouble. It was this association with Irving that lead to the rather pedestrian Arrol-Johnston becoming involved with the world's fastest car.

My father took me down to see the 'Bluebird' at Dumfries. There was little activity on the other assembly lines. A few 'twelves' were being produced as well as the 15.9, and work on 'Bluebird' could not have employed more than six men. The name 'Arrol-Aster' was already painted on the car's tail fin.

It is questionable whether Beardmore was very interested in the company during this period. The ghost of the 'Victory' inhibited the design team, who were in any case totally dominated by Pullinger and his ultra-conservative policies. The only flicker of former enthusiasm had come in 1922, when, for some inexplicable reason, Beardmore experimented once again with a two-stroke engine, offering a 73mm x 98mm engine and chassis at the 1922 Motor Show. The price alone was enough to dissuade customers. The whole project sounded like one of Beardmore's flights of fancy, with Pullinger making certain of its extinction by raising the price.

However, Pullinger's bid to achieve the ultimate in orthodoxy had left him with nowhere to go. The cars lacked vitality and sparkle; sound engineering practice was not enough. For its last six years the company drifted along without any apparent purpose except that of extinction. The change to overhead valves had come too late.

Make	ARROL-JOHNSTON				
Year	1898	1905-07	1906-09	1907-09	1907-09
Model	Dogcart	18	12/15	16/25	24/30
Factory	Camlachie		Paisley		
Nº CYL	2	2	2	4 in pairs	4 in pairs
Bore	84.4	121	108	105	108
Stroke	109	165	165	125	127
cc capacity	3230	3800	3024	4330	4655
Valves	Auto inlet	Auto inlet	Auto inlet	IOE	IOE
BHP					
Maker's rating	12	18	14.5	27.3	28.9
Carburation					
Cooling system	Thermo syphon	Thermo syphon	Thermo syphon	Thermo syphon	Thermo syphon
Lubrication system	Splash	Splash	Splash	Forced	Forced
Gear box	4 Σ R	4 Σ R	4 Σ R	4 Σ R	4 Σ R
Rear axle ratio	4:1		4:1	4:1	4:1
Transmission	Chain	Shaft & bevel	Shaft & bevel	Shaft & bevel	Shaft & bevel
Suspension F/R	e ½e	½e ½e	½e ½e	½e ½e	½e ½e
Wheel base length	5'5"	7'8"	8'9"-10'3"	9'6"	9'6"-9'8"
Track width	4'6"	4'4"	4'4½"	4'4½"	4'4½"-4'6"
Weight (cwt)			19	19½	25
Tyre size: front		815x105	810x90	815x105	875x105
Tyre size: rear			810x90		
Wheels	wood fixed	wood spokes or wire	wood spokes or wire	wood spokes or wire	wood spokes or wire
Price (£): chassis					
Price (£): complete			450	510	600

1907-08	1908-14	1911-13	1912-14	1912-13	1914	1915 prototype
38/45	15.9	23.9	11.9	15.9	20.9	17.9
	Paisley Dumfries	Dumfries				
4 in pairs	4 in pairs	6 in pairs	4 in pairs	4 in pairs	4 in pairs	4 in pairs
136	80	80	69	80	91	85
152	120	120	120	140	140	140
8826	2409	3619	1795	2815	3642	2724
IOE	SV	SV	SV	SV	SV	SV
	15·9	15·9	15·9	15·9	15·9	15·9
	Zenith	White & poppe	Stethands	White & poppe	Zenith	Zenith
Thermo syphon	Thermo syphon	Thermo syphon	Thermo syphon	Thermo syphon	Thermo syphon	Thermo syphon
Forced	Forced	Forced	Forced	Forced	Forced	Forced
$4 \Sigma R$	$4 \Sigma R$	$4 \Sigma R$	$4 \Sigma R$	$4 \Sigma R$	$4 \Sigma R$	$4 \Sigma R$
4:1	4:1 4.25:1	4:1	4:1	4:1	4:1	4:1
Shaft & bevel	Shaft & spiral bevel	Spiral bevel	Spiral bevel	Spiral bevel	Spiral bevel	Spiral bevel
½e ½e	½e double e	½e double e	½e double e	½e double e	½e double e	½e double e
16'5"	9'6"	10'4½"	9'4"	9'3"-10'3"	10'3"	9'9"
5'4½"	4'7"	4'4¾"	4'8"	4'8"	4'8"	4'7"
	17	19½	15	15	17	14
920x120	760x90	820x120	760x90	815x105	820x120	815x105
spokes or wire	steel disc detachable	steel spoke	steel disc	steel disc	steel disc	steel disc
	625-725		285			

Make	ARROL-JOHNSTON				
Year	1918-19	1920-21	1922-23	1923-28	1924-25
Model	Victory	15.9	15.9	15.9	14
Factory	Dumfries				
Nº CYL	4 mono block	4 in pairs	4 mono block	4	4
Bore	75 80	80	80	80	75
Stroke	150 140	120	130	130	120
cc capacity	2652/2815	2413	2616	2616	2121
Valves	OHC	SV	SV	SV	SV
BHP	40	22	36	36	
Maker's rating	13.9	15.9	15.9	15.9	14
Carburation	Zenith	Zenith	Cox Atmos	Cox Atmos	Zenith
Cooling system	Pump	T.S.	T.S	Pump	Pump
Lubrication system	Pressure	Pressure	Pressure	Pressure	Pressure
Gear box	4 Σ R	4 Σ R	4 Σ R	4 Σ R	4 Σ R
Rear axle ratio		4:1 4·25:1	4·25:1	4·25:1	4·5:1
Transmission	Helical bevel	Spiral bevel	Torque tube spiral bevel	Torque tube spiral bevel	Torque tube spiral bevel
Suspension F/R	½e cant.	½e double e	½e ½e	½e ½e	½e ½e
Wheel base length	10'	9'9"	10'0	10'0	9'9"
Track width	4'8"	4'8"	4'8"	4'8"	4'8"
Weight (cwt)	12	23	23	23	23
Tyre size: front	820x120	815x105	815x105	820x120	765x105
Tyre size: rear					
Wheels	Artillery	Disc	Disc	Dunlop Steel Spoke	Steel Spoke
Price (£): chassis	600	525	575	450	325
Price (£): complete	700	625T 725S	650T 850S	550T 695 750S	398T 559S

1924-27	1925-26	1925-28	1927-28	1927-28	1928
Empire 20	12	Dominium 15.9	12	24/70*	15/40
4	4	4	4	6	4
89.75	69.5	80	69.5	80	80
130	110	120 130	110	115	120
3290	1670	2413/2616	1670	3470	2413
SV	SV	OHV	OHV	OHV	OHV
50					40
20	11.9	15.9	20	21	15.9
Zenith	Zenith	Zenith	Zenith	Zenith	Zenith
Pump	Pump	Pump	Pump	Pump	Pump
Pressure	Pressure	Pressure	Pressure	Pressure	Pressure
4 Σ R	4 Σ R	4 Σ R	4 Σ R	4 Σ R	4 Σ R
4·25:1	4·54:1 4·5:1	4·16:1 4·53:1	4·5:1	4·16:1	4·16:1
Torque tube spiral bevel	Shaft & spiral bevel	Torque tube spiral bevel	Shaft & spiral bevel	Torque tube spiral bevel	Torque tube spiral bevel
½e ½e	½e ¼e	½e ½e	½e ¼e	½e cant.	½e ½e
10'6"	9'6"	9'9"	9'6"	12'3"	9'9"
4'8"	4'3½"	4'8"	4'3½"	4'8"	4'8"
23	25¼	23		23	23
820x120	28x4.95	30x5.25	28x4.95	33x6.75	31x5.25
Steel Spoke	Disc	Artillery	Artillery	Artillery	Artillery
425	360	315			380
498T 7255	425/435	425T			425T

*Virtually a 24/70 Aster but with 21/60 engine bored out to 80mm

During 1928, sleeve valve aster cars were marketed under the Arrol-Johnston badge 21/60, 24/70, 17/50, 23/70

GALLOWAY
MOTORS LTD

The Galloway light car – the Fiat connection

GALLOWAY Motors Ltd was established in 1920. The directors were William Beardmore, Thomas Pullinger, Miss Dorothée Pullinger, R. H. Ballantyne, Charles Penfold Pullinger, and E. E. Leverett who owned a motor sales and distribution business in London. The capital was £200,000 and they took over the business of the Galloway Engineering Company Ltd. An interesting point about the factory at Tongland was that the electrical power was supplied by water turbines in the River Dee.

Apart from the manufacture of Beardmore 'BHP' aero engines during World War I, the Tongland factory produced aircraft wings, tail assemblies and gun mountings, as well as complete aircraft (some of which were still being manufactured at the Tongland factory during 1920/21). Production had been drastically cut and the necessity of keeping the factory busy was urgent. Pullinger was in a serious situation where he had to do something to

Galloway Drop Head Coupé.

justify his decision to break the Beardmore control and to redress the 'Victory' failure. Having refused to enter the sports car market, he decided to try his hand at a light car.

Beardmore's long-standing association with Fiat provided the necessary design expertise. Although a suitable engine in the shape of the Brown-designed 1656cc SV was available, complete with patterns and all tooling, Pullinger was no innovator, preferring to follow well-trodden paths. In this case the path led to the Fiat Tipo 510. One can only speculate whether there was anyone at Arrol-Johnston capable of designing, or perhaps *allowed* to design, a new car.

Dorothée Pullinger, who had been born in France while her father was working for Darracq at Suresne, was appointed manager. The factory employed mainly female labour. The Galloway light car was a nice enough car, although it suffered from increased weight in the conversion; and whatever sparkle the Fiat may have possessed was totally lost in the Galloway copy. The car was listed at 10.5hp 1460cc SV, the same as the Tipo 510, and carried a very smart but heavy coupé body which the company advertised as a 'doctor's car'. In open two-seater form, two cars competed in the 1922 Scottish six-day trial without loss of any marks. Unfortunately this success failed to make any impression on the market. The problem that Galloway and all other cars in the same class faced was competition from William Morris. In the case of Galloway there was a difference of about £100. The enterprise lasted for only two years as a separate entity. In 1922 both Galloway and Arrol-Johnston were suffering from a shortage of orders. Long overdue rationalisation took place. The Tongland factory was closed and the production of Galloway cars was transferred to Heathhall where it lasted until 1928.

In 1923 the bore was increased, giving a capacity of 1483cc. In 1924 an 8cwt van was introduced, the bore being increased again. Later in the same year the bore for private cars was increased, which gave a capacity of 1669cc. Pullinger might as well have used the side-valve Beardmore engine in the first place. The performance, however, remained mediocre. At the end of 1926 the engine had overhead valves and was just a small Arrol-Johnston. However, to be fair the Galloway never set out to have a brisk performance; it was intended to fill the roll of second car in a two-car household. It was meant for doctors' rounds or shopping expeditions, or as a local runabout. The market for that type of car was full to overflowing and the slavish policy of copying an existing design diminished the car's appeal and robbed it of any distinction.

Make	GALLOWAY				
Year	1920-22	1923-25	1924	1924-26	1927-28
Model	10/20	10/20	Van 8cwt	12/20	12/50
Factory	Tongland	Heathall			
Nº CYL	4	4	4	4	4
Bore	65	66·5	66·5	69·5	69·5
Stroke	110	110	110	110	110
cc capacity	1460	1528	1528	1669	1669
Valves	SV	SV	SV.	SV	OHV
BHP	20 @ 2000				20 @ 2000
Maker's rating	10·9	10·9	10·9	11·9	11·9
Carburation	Zenith	Zenith	Zenith	Zenith	Zenith
Cooling System	pump	pump	pump	pump	pump
Lubrication System	pressure	pressure	pressure	pressure	pressure
Gear box	3 Σ R	4 Σ R	4 Σ R	4 Σ R	4 Σ R
Rear axle ratio	4·2:1	4·2:1	4·9:1	4·9:1	4·9:1
Transmission	spiral bevel	spiral bevel	spiral bevel	spiral bevel	spiral bevel
Suspension F/R	½e ¼e	½e ¼e	½e ¼e	½e ¼e	½e ¼e
Wheel base	8'6"/9'4"	9'6"	9'4"	9'6"	9'6"
Track width	4'3½"	4'3½"	4'1"	4'3½"	4'3½"
Weight (cwt)	18				
Tyre size: front	710x80	28x4·95	710x90	28x4·95	29x4·95
Tyre size: rear					
Wheels	disc	disc	disc	disc	disc
Price (£): chassis	225				
Price (£): complete	265/360		265	275	360

THE AUSTRIAN
CONNECTION

The Austrian connection – Ferdinand Porsche – Austro Daimler –
the 120hp engine developed to 160hp – Internment of the Austrian
engineers – the 230 'BHP' – Halford's contribution –
John Siddeley and the 'Puma' engine – metallurgical developments

CAR production ceased in 1914 and all energies were transferred to the production of the Beardmore aero engine. Sometime around 1912 Beardmore obtained a licence to manufacture the Austro Daimler 90hp and 120hp six-cylinder aero engines and it appears that the London agents for Austro Daimler cars may have acted as the go-between. The agency was held by George Allsworth and Francis M. Luther, and it was the latter who brought the manufacturing drawings out of Austria.

Luther also brought out a team of Austrian Engineers who designed the various modifications, including an increase in bore size, which eventually boosted the output to 160hp and 185hp.

It is more than likely that they laid out the design of the enlarged 230hp engine before they were interned as enemy aliens in 1914. The agreement with Austro Daimler was in the name of 'Beardmore engine works, Dalmuir', not in the name of 'Arrol-Johnston' who, with the Galloway Engineering

Beardmore 160hp engine. (© Royal Air Force Museum)

Company, were destined to be subcontractors to the Beardmore aero engine works – a fact which may have caused Pullinger some unease.

The Austro Daimler aero engine was designed by Dr Ing Ferdinand Porsche in 1910. It was an outstanding six-in-line and in its original form had positively opened and closed valves operated by push/pull rods from a camshaft in the crankcase. By 1911 the bore and stroke were 130mm x 175mm, giving a capacity of 13.9 litres and an output of 120bhp at 1200 rev/min (the 90hp engine does not appear to have been manufactured by Beardmore).

Between 1911 and 1914 it was one of the best-selling engines and it set a standard for aero engine design for many years to come. The Beardmore version had several modifications, including dual ignition and twin carburettors. By that time the desmodromic system had been dropped by Porsche and the valves, four per cylinder, were operated by overhead camshaft. But this design was not available to Beardmore.

The Beardmore engine retained a modified desmodromic system. The cylinder liners were closed at one end to form a flattened dome. This was threaded and screwed into the cylinder head which had a similar profile, thus forming metal to metal contact. This overcame the problem of porosity in the cast cylinder head, but increased the problem of heat transfer from the exhaust valve. The valve seats and guides were machined after the assembly.

The increased bores of the 160hp (bore 142mm/stroke 176mm) and 185hp engines did give room for increased valve diameters, but burnt valves were an growing problem. Even in the 1930s Joe Craig of Norton Motor Cycles said that the exhaust valve was the limiting factor in increasing power output.

Several thousand Beardmore aero engines, now rated at 160hp, saw service in World War I and in this form it was most successful. In 1915 the Beardmore Aero Engine Company was registered. They had already broken away from Porsche's original design by increasing the bore to 143mm, giving a capacity of 16.4 litres with a rating of 185bhp at 1450 rev/min. However, this had stretched the design to its limit and work on the larger 230hp engine was already underway. This engine was later to become the 'BHP', but, as stated on page 44, its origins probably lay with the Austrian engineers.

The 160hp engine, which continued in production, was mainly used in the FE 2b aircraft. In 1916 Lieutenant (later Major) Frank Bernard Halford, previously with the Aeronautical Inspection Department (AID) at Farnborough, was recalled from duties in France and given the job of quality control and establishing an AID inspectorate at Arrol-Johnston. Halford has been given the credit for the design and development of the larger 'BHP' engine, but there is no record of official instructions to this effect. In fact all design details carry the signature of 'T. C. Pullinger', which implies that he was Chief Engineer in charge of the project. Likewise, all patents were in the name of Pullinger and the Beardmore Aero Engine Company. While the actual details of the engine had many typically French touches, which is not surprising considering that both Pullinger and Halford were heavily influenced by French practice and the basic design was of continental origin, there are certainly no signs of any bias towards the designs of any French aero engine manufacturers, and in particular Hispano Suiza.

Frank Bernard Halford joined the Royal Flying Corps straight from school. He became a flying instructor at Brooklands and in 1914 joined the AID as an 'engine examiner'. Halford had had no technical training, nor did he possess any academic qualifications. He did attend a diploma course in mechanical engineering at Nottingham University, but failed it. At the outbreak of war he was sent to France to examine the French aero engine situation. He was enthusiastic about the Hispano Suiza engine, which he considered to be an outstanding design, and tried hard to persuade the War Office to take up a manufacturing licence.

Whitehall was not about to take advice from a 21 year-old 2nd lieutenant and in due course he was posted to Arrol-Johnston as AID inspector. But it was highly unlikely that the domineering Pullinger would regard the young man any differently to the War Office and entrust the design of a technically-advanced engine to an unqualified and inexperienced individual.

At the time of Halford's arrival a prototype of the new 230hp engine was running but giving unsatisfactory results, being unreliable and down on power. The design followed the general principals of the original Porsche design: the cylinders were forged steel surrounded by tubular welded sheet steel water jackets with seals to retain the water at top and bottom. As before, the cylinders were screwed into the head.

The bore was 145mm and the stroke 190.5mm. The capacity was 19 litres and it was rated at 230hp. The desmodromic system was dropped in favour of an overhead camshaft, but the original two-valve head was retained. It is probable that the exhaust valves could no longer cope with the heat flow.

In spite of the fact that he had no authority, Halford became involved in the development work. There can be little doubt that he knew about Theo Biggs' 1912 engine, and with considerable help from the drawing office he produced a new cylinder head with two exhaust valves and one large inlet valve per cylinder. The head was of cast iron and appears to have consisted of two blocks of three cylinders. At that time Halford, lacking technical or academic qualifications, could not have created the design himself. Instead he had an intuitive knack of spotting the cause of trouble and also the gift of farsightedness. Halford was always one jump ahead and really came into his own years later with the design of jet engines. He deserves full credit for the idea of adapting Biggs' three-valve design to the troubled 230bhp engine.

There must have been strong arguments in favour of the three-valve design. It solved the heat dissipation problem from the exhaust valves, and this suggests that at least one of Biggs' engines had been built and had given very good results on test. Due to design modifications, the 'BHP' was rated at 250bhp. Oddly enough there is no record of Biggs' involvement, although his services were available to the Beardmore Aero Engine Company.

The new cylinder head and other modifications to improve reliability were sufficient for the engine to be accepted into service. All attempts to use aluminium instead of cast iron failed because of porosity.

As we have seen, the engine was named the rather confusing 'BHP', which stood for 'Beardmore' and 'Pullinger', with 'Halford' perhaps conveniently providing the 'H'. After the war the claims commission awarded Halford only 25 per cent of the credit, leaving 75 per cent unaccounted for. This was mostly claimed by Pullinger but it left the question of true authorship unanswered. The total amount of the award was the then not inconsiderable sum of £20,000.

It is doubtful if Pullinger contributed much if anything to the design of the 'BHP'. It is true that his signature appears on all drawings, as chief engineer, but that is more in keeping with his character than his ability as a design engineer. He had had no prior experience with aero engine design and lacked the necessary originality and imagination.

His great mistake was in not obtaining the services of a qualified aero engine designer after the Austrian engineers had been interned. Having also failed to replace Biggs and blocked the appointment of Brown, Pullinger appears to have been conceited enough to imagine that he could do the job himself. To increase production of the new 'BHP' additional manufacturing facilities were put in hand and a new factory was built at Tongland for the Galloway Engineering Company. However, Pullinger failed to appreciate both the urgency and the large number of engines required.

The result in both cars and aero engines was disastrous: most of his time must have been taken up with running the factory and attending to the vast production of the 160hp and 185hp engines.

At that time Beardmore engines were considered to be the best 'in-line' water-cooled engines available to the Royal Flying Corps (renamed the Royal Air Force in 1918 when it moved from army and naval control to separate command).

The manufacture and development of engines seems to have been a very fragmented affair. The Beardmore Aero Engine Company appears to have had little or no control over Arrol-Johnston, but they built the 160hp engine at their Speedwell factory at Coatbridge and also at Crossley Motors in Manchester. However, the appointment of Crossley as a subcontractor seems to have been authorised by the Ministry of Munitions without anyone being designated responsibility for liaison, or even determining which company to liaise with. The Aero Engine Company's design offices were busy with a very much larger engine, and the involvement of Theo Biggs and Frank E. Baker's team has never been explained. Nevertheless, thousands of 160hp and 185hp engines were produced and fitted into an unbelievable number of airframes. If these three companies had not achieved such a high production rate, the RFC would not have been able to achieve air superiority. The importance of this very successful engine cannot be over emphasised.

Towards the end of the war the Beardmore aero engine was rated at 185hp for a weight of 650lbs and it is estimated that the 160hp and 185hp engines carried more bombs over Germany and German-occupied territories than any other aerial power unit. By the end of the war the 'Beardmore' name was changed to 'Galloway'.

Frank Halford eventually joined De Havilland and designed the 'Cirrus' engines and the famous 'Gypsy' engines.* He also designed and built the supercharged Halford specials of Brooklands' fame, but that is another story. During his time with Beardmore he was involved with the Galloway Engineering Company where he is credited with reworking the Siddeley 'Puma', raising the capacity to 20.7 litres and using the stronger crankshaft of the Galloway 'Adriatic'. Rated at 335bhp at 1600 rev/min and named the 'Nimbus', Galloway also produced the 'Adriatic', itself a 'BHP' with the stronger crankshaft, and also a twelve-cylinder 'V' engine, the Galloway 'Atlantic', rated at 500bhp.

Interestingly, the Galloway 'Adriatic' was used in the DH 9a, a commercial passenger conversion of the DH 9 Bomber. Six passengers were accommodated in a cabin amidships whilst the pilot sat in an open cockpit on top and at the rear of the machine. As some cynic remarked, 'When it crashed, the pilot would be the only survivor able to give account of the accident'. In the meantime the Beardmore Aero Engine Company at Dalmuir was working on an 840bhp 'Cyclone', a giant inverted six-in-line of 8.5 inch bore and 12 inch stroke; and also developing high-speed lightweight engines of the diesel and semi-diesel type, all of which after 1918 were designed by A. E. Chorlton.

A new tactical bomber, the DH 9, was being produced. Unfortunately the Galloway Engineering Company, due to delays in the construction of the factory, was unable to meet the demand for 'BHP' engines.

It was realised too late that the Tongland factory could not be completed in time to meet delivery demands for the 'BHP' and a desperate attempt was

---

* The 'Gypsy' engine is reputed to have been half a Renault V8 and Geoffrey De Havilland bought as many ex-airforce surplus V8s as possible.

made to transfer production to Crossley Motors. However, the war ended before Crossley made any engines, and the Tongland factory was only completed after 1918.

Beardmore Aero Engine Company was the main contractor. The responsibility for the production of engines was theirs and they must take the blame. But without doubt the culprits were Pullinger and Beardmore. The former was obsessed with building an empire and unable to recognise any problem arising from his own faulty administration; the latter, as chairman of Arrol-Johnston, was the only link between that company and the Aero Engine Company. He failed to acquaint himself with the situation and failed to provide any coherent policy or overall control, all of which led to the loss of the manufacturing contract.

An astute businessman called John Siddeley, who was not averse to a little cunning opportunism, moved in to exploit the situation and obtained a large contract for quantity production of the engine. Siddeley-Deasy also had a great deal more space than Arrol-Johnston and Galloway. Figures speak for themselves:

Galloway Engineering ('BHP')	order	560	delivered	94
Crossley Motors	order	500	delivered	0
Siddeley ('Puma')	order	11,500	delivered	4288

All uncompleted orders were cancelled after the Armistice.

Siddeley was assured by Pullinger, in the presence of Beardmore, that the porosity problem with the aluminium cylinder head had been overcome, but after experiencing a rejection rate of about 80 per cent he pulled out of the agreement and would only continue if given a free hand with a redesign.

To assist Siddeley, Major F. M. Green (no relation to Gustavus Green and Green aero engines) was detached from Farnborough to serve as Chief Engineer (aero) of Siddeley-Deasy. Green had no instruction to increase the power, but he was confident that 300bhp could be obtained. Further redesign of the cylinder heads was undertaken and the engine was renamed the 'Puma'. Unfortunately various problems arose, such as porosity of the cylinder heads when the engine was rated at 300bhp, and it was derated to 240, although a few 290bhp units did go into service. (Cylinder head porosity was one of the limiting factors in obtaining high engine performance at that time. It was a metallurgical problem that would be solved slowly as casting and alloy techniques improved.) Hispano Suiza overcame the problem by stove enamelling the cylinder heads.

Siddeley also took with him John Lloyd who had been head of the stress department at Farnborough, and S. D. Heron who was later to become famous as the inventor of the Heron head.

By the time the 'Puma' reached the service it bore little resemblance to the 'BHP'. The cylinder head was cast aluminium, as were the water jackets, and few components, if any, were interchangeable. Despite Halford's warning to the authorities his complaints were ignored, much to his anger and frustration. No one seems to have paid any attention to the differences between the two engines until it was discovered that the Siddeley-Deasy version would not fit into an air frame designed for a 'BHP'. Crossley Motors' poor performance was due to the order being for the Siddeley-designed 'BHP', under the misapprehension that the engines were interchangeable (the use of 'bhp' and 'BHP' was coincidental, but nonetheless confusing). This extraordinary situation was mainly due to the authorities who ignored Halford's warnings, but it was also due to Beardmore's incompetence. He was well aware of the agreement between the government supply board and John Siddeley's *carte blanche* agreement which allowed him to do anything he wanted. Beardmore failed to make sure that he was adequately protected from patent infringement, and the government failed to see or control the consequences.

Pullinger, meanwhile, failed to appreciate the need not only to solve outstanding technical problems, but to get the 'BHP'-designed engine into production as rapidly as possible in order to forestall Siddeley-Deasy. Halford continued to issue warnings, but John Siddeley was too smart for them. Having larger manufacturing capacity than Arrol-Johnston and Galloway, he continued his secret agenda.

Many of Siddeley's modifications were designed to avoid payment of royalties. Improvements, like the use of aluminium water jackets which eliminated water seal problems, were patented so that Beardmore could not use them, even though, under patent law, Beardmore was more entitled to their use. The repositioning of the engine mountings, along with dimensional changes to various components, ruled out the 'BHP' as an alternative power unit. To add to the confusion, Arrol-Johnston became subcontractors to Galloway, who immediately changed the name 'BHP' to Galloway 'Adriatic'.

As a result Siddeley ended up with an excellent aero engine without having to pay licence fees, and of course without competition. As one of P. G. Wodehouse's characters used to say, 'Never give a sucker an even break'. The 'Adriatic/Puma', as it was known, was an outstanding design and it remained in production even after the end of World War I.

Halford then transferred to Galloway where he worked on a V12 engine consisting of two 'Adriatic' cylinder blocks on a common crankshaft. This engine, the Galloway 'Atlantic', was designed to answer the demand for a 'bomb Berlin bus'. Both Vickers and Handley-Page had large enough aeroplanes, but the Rolls-Royce 'Eagle' engines lacked enough power to carry an adequate bombload. The Rolls-Royce 'Condor', meanwhile, was insufficiently advanced for use.

Siddeley-Deasy also produced a V12 consisting of two 'Puma' blocks on a common crankcase. For some reason they infringed on Galloway's nomenclature by calling it the 'Pacific'. Both engines were rated at 500hp, although some authorities claimed 550hp. All these engines had the same bore and stroke (*ie* bore 145mm and stroke 190mm).

The war ended before any of these V12 engines were used. The Galloway 'Atlantic', however, achieved some notoriety, being the favoured power plant which, when installed in fast hulls, was used by Chicago bootleggers to transport their merchandise across the Canadian lakes. Thus equipped, they were able to show a clean pair of heels to the United States coastguards.

The loss of the manufacturing contract for 'Adriatic' engines to Siddeley-Deasy was a serious blow to Beardmore. In the immediate term it cost the company the initiative as the leading manufacturers of in-line water-cooled aero engines, and in the long term it was faced with competition from a better organised company and a more developed engine.

Meanwhile Arrol-Johnston's associate, Aster Engineering Company, was busy manufacturing Gustavus Green's beautifully-made aero engines: the six-in-line water-cooled OHC 120 x 152mm, rated at 120 bhp. These engines were robust and simple, but the weight of 450lbs was a problem and they were mainly used in fast, small boats for the Admiralty and in small airships.

The search for increased horsepower was not confined to Britain. By 1917 the remarkable Porsche had raised the power of the OHC Austro Daimler engine to 225bhp without changing the bore size.

The famous 'Sopwith Pup' was powered by Clerget or Le Rhone engines, both only 80hp. Later, Clerget were producing 130hp and these were used in the 'Sopwith Camel'. Not all these improvements were due to design. Until 1914 the only steel available to engineers was high or low carbon steel with a small nickel addition. Low carbon steel could be rolled into thin sheets and was malleable. High carbon steel had greater strength and hardness, but became brittle at the top end. Chrome alloys were in use, mainly in the manufacture of armour plate, but there were serious unresolved problems in its manufacture which made it liable to brittleness. An independent metalurgical consultant named Harry Brearley* solved these problems and incidentally discovered stainless steel at the same time. Under his guidance, Brown Bayleys Steelworks Ltd of Sheffield produced thousands of reliable crankshaft forgings, so that by 1916 practically all aero engine crankshafts were made from nickel chrome alloy (prior to that, the crankshaft of one aero engine had an estimated working life of four hours).

---

* Brearley's research into the manufacturing processes of steelmaking improved not only armour plate, gun barrels and crankshafts, but all steel products, and can be regarded as a major breakthrough.

ASTER ENGINEERING COMPANY (1913) LTD

Aster Engineering Company (1913) Ltd – Green aero engines

ASTER was originally the licensee of Ateliers de Construction Mechanique l'Aster in France, manufacturers of proprietary engines to many French car builders, both small and large, and second in importance to De Dion. The company was established in England in 1899 when Sydney Dawson Begbie obtained a manufacturing licence for the Begbie Manufacturing Company at Wembley. The company was restructured financially several times, and it was in 1913 that Beardmore is thought to have instigated the purchase of a large shareholding by Arrol-Johnston. In the 1913 restructuring Aster had a nominal capital of £80,000 in £1 shares, but this was augmented in 1919 by the issue of 100,000 eight per cent cumulative preference £1 shares. Aster was not, at that stage, building its own cars, although it marketed an Aries chassis with an Aster engine and British bodywork. Primarily engine builders, Aster produced stationary electric generator sets and pumps for Merryweather fire engines. The company had also been manufacturing

18/50 Aster, 1922. (National Motor Museum)

Gustavus Green's 50hp four-cylinder water-cooled aero engine since 1906, and in 1913 it was working on Green's prize-winning design for a six-cylinder in-line aero engine.

The Aster company had established a reputation for high-quality workmanship and the Green engine was noted for the excellence of its finish. It was doubtless this expertise which Beardmore required for the manufacture of the Austro Daimler engine. The acquisition of a large shareholding, or any other agreement, did not include control of policy; this seems to have remained firmly in Sydney Begbie's hands.

In 1920 Aster produced an exciting four-cylinder DOHC engine 65mm x 150mm 1992cc, although it did not seem to have had any appeal to the users of proprietary engines. Perhaps the price was too high or the bore/stroke ratio was unsuitable. In 1922 Aster entered the car market with a six-cylinder 2618cc OHV chassis designated 18/50. The design was modern; the engine and four-speed gearbox was in unit construction, with dry plate clutch, four wheel brakes, automatic chassis lubrication and cantilever rear suspension. As with the aero engines, quality was of an extremely high standard. The chassis, suspension and torque tube followed the same layout as the 'Victory', although the wheel base of the 18/50 was six inches longer at ten feet six inches. The track was the same and the rear axle ratio was 4.2:1, identical to the Arrol-Johnston. The similarity between the Aster and the 'Victory' may be coincidence or evidence of technical co-operation. Both Arrol-Johnston and Aster were competing for a market that was already overcrowded and shrinking fast. The Aster had a more sporting appeal and a very high standard of workmanship combined with a higher price tag.

In 1924 the engine capacity of the 18/50 was increased to 2888cc and named the 20/55. The 24/70 Arrol-Johnston appears to be a bored-out version (3468cc) of the 20/55 Aster. In 1925 the 21/60 model was produced and the company received a publicity boost when HRH the Duke of York purchased a sports version. This car was capable of well over 70mph. In 1926 the company abandoned OHV, except for the 21/60, in favour of sleeve valves. The bore was increased, giving a capacity of 3468cc. Just to keep the Humber syndrome alive, Theo Biggs joined Aster in 1926, later returning with them to Dumfries.

In 1927 neither Aster nor Arrol-Johnston were in good financial condition and the two were amalgamated under one management. Pullinger had retired, Willie Lowe succeeded him, and Beardmore was again the principal shareholder, now joined by Sydney Begbie and Edward Claude Shakespear Clench of Aster. The two companies were amalgamated into Arrol-Aster Engineering Company, with the factory at Heathhall. The Aster factory at Hendon was taken over by Beardmore Motor Company as a service station for the taxis, then as an assembly depot, and finally in 1932 as the manufacturing centre.

ARROL-ASTER
(1927) LTD

Arrol-Aster (1927) Ltd – sleeve valves – wobble shaft – supercharger

WITH the amalgamation the capital was increased to £200,000 by the creation of a further 100,000 six per cent cumulative preference shares of £1 each. The directors were William Beardmore, Thomas Pullinger (now retired and living in Jersey), James David George Hendry, William Lowe, Robert Hendry Wheeler, Sydney Begbie and Edward Clench. The first four were from Arrol-Johnston and the last three from Aster. Pullinger resigned as a director soon after the formation. Of the existing 100,000 shares Beardmore held 60,579, John Robertson Johnston (any relationship with Arrol-Johnston is unknown) held 25,796, Pullinger 12,471, and the balance was held by the other five.

Sydney Begbie acted as liquidator for Aster, which was sold to Arrol-Johnston for £90,000; Edward Clench was in charge of technical development and design.

A final burst of activity, rather like that of a dying star, took place in 1927 when the Arrol-Aster was born. The Arrol-Aster was the largest car ever built in Scotland and thanks to Aster's coach building design, which replaced

Eight-cylinder Arrol-Aster.

the rather stuffy lines of the Arrol-Johnston, it was the best-looking car of its time. However, where the old company suffered from a lack of innovation, the new company had a bit too much of it, some in the untried category. The amalgamation did not mean that production had been rationalised – far from it. The Galloway name was retained, but the car was the same as the 12hp Arrol-Johnston and the eight models covered a price range from £360 to £1200. These were the 12hp Galloway, now with OHV engine, the 12hp Arrol-Johnston, the 15/40 OHV 'Dominian', and the 24/70 Arrol-Johnston. Arrol-Aster continued the 21/60 OHV Aster, and also introduced the 17/50, 21/60 and 24/70 Burt McCullum sleeve-valve engines under the Arrol-Aster name. In 1927 the 23/70 straight-eight engine was introduced. The bore was 67.5mm, but the stroke was 110mm. At the same time the stroke of the 17/50 was reduced to 110mm.

By 1929 all the OHV cars had been dropped and only the two 110mm stroke Arrol-Asters remained. All the engines were now six or eight-cylinders with sleeve valves driven by an unusual operating mechanism called a wobble shaft. Ever since the first car was built, engineers have searched for an alternative to the poppet valve, rotary valves, sliding valves, pistons and sleeves. The list of patents is endless,

Sleeve-valve wobble shaft. (Courtesy of Mitchell Library)

but of all these the sleeve valve was the most promising and its eventual application in aero engines was an outstanding success. The wobble shaft was an ingenious way of operating the sleeve, the path described by the sleeve being an almost perfect circle and largely eliminating the accelerations and decelerations of other types of mechanisms. In essence the wobble shaft was a small crankshaft with the connecting rod journals oblique to the axis of the main bearings. It was built up from identical sections bolted together, the join being covered by a sleeve which formed the journal for a main bearing. The connecting rods were triangular in shape, the base of the triangle formed the big end bearing, while the apex carried a ball joint which was attached to the sleeve. The shaft which ran at half engine speed could be run up to 2000 rev/min before out-of-balance forces became a serious problem. That meant the engine could be taken up to 4000 rev/min, although problems with cracked sleeves effectively limited the engine to 3500 rev/min.

The advantages were an efficient design of combustion chamber, smoothness and quiet operation and no tappets to adjust. The main disadvantage was the limitation of maximum rev/min. The disadvantages of the poppet valve were rapidly being overcome. It was a cheaper system to manufacture and the search for higher-power outputs could only be achieved by higher rev/min. The sleeve-valve Aster was never designed to be a high-output sports car engine, and the only way that power output could be increased whilst remaining within the restricted revolution range was by fitting a supercharger.

A Cozette vane-type supercharger, running at a pressure of 6lbs per square inch, was installed on the 2.3-litre six-cylinder 17/50. With increased cost and complexity, this was only partially successful. It was belt-driven from a pulley on the end of the wobble shaft and the low-speed torque was improved, but the engine was unable to benefit from the improved breathing which would have been advantageous at high engine speeds. Leverett and Kearton Ltd, who handled the London sales, were the instigators of the supercharged 17/50 model which was introduced in 1929. The cars appeared in several sporting events including the Alpine trial, and the Ulster TT with E. R. Hall at the wheel. However, they only met with moderate success and with this last burst of energy the star of Arrol-Aster finally expired.

Beardmore had at last achieved his ambition to build a large sporting car. However, by the time he had the car on the market, that market was almost non-existent, decimated by the financial slump of the late 1920s. His search for an engine design which would put him ahead of his competitors had lead him up a blind alley; the wobble shaft in this instance turned out to be just a mechanical curiosity. Ironically the only car which could have been developed to meet Beardmore's sporting ambitions was the 2.8 litre Arrol-Johnston 'Victory'.

Make	ASTER			
Year	1923-24	1925-29	1926-28	1926-28
Model	18/50	20/55	21/60	24/70
Factory	Wembley			
Nº CYL	6	6	6	6
Bore	69·5	73	75	80
Stroke	115	115	115	115
cc capacity	2618	2889	3045	3468
Valves	OHV	OHV	OHV/sleeve	sleeve
BHP	55 @ 3000			
Maker's rating			20·9	
Carburation				
Cooling System	Pump	Pump	Pump	Pump
Lubrication System	Pressure	Pressure	Pressure	Pressure
Gear box	4 Σ R	4 Σ R	4 Σ R	4 Σ R
Rear axle ratio	4·2:1	4·2:1	4·16:1	4·16:1
Transmission	Torque Tube Spiral Bevel	Torque Tube Spiral Bevel	Torque Tube Spiral Bevel	Torque Tubel Spiral Bevel
Suspension F/R	½e cant.	½e cant.	½e cant.	½e cant.
Wheel base length	10'6"	10'11"	11'3"	12'3"
Track width	4'8½"	4'8½"	4'8½"	4'8½"
Weight (cwt)				
Tyre size: front	820x120	32x6.2	32x6.2	33x6.75
Tyre size: rear				
Wheels	Wire	Wire	Wire	Wire
Price (£): chassis				785
Price (£): complete	850 1015		750OHV 810S	950 1250

Make	ARROL-ASTER		
Year	1927-29	1927-31	1928-30
Model	17/50	23-70	17/50
Factory	Wembley/ Dumfries	Dumfries	
Nº CYL	6	8	6
Bore	67·5	67·5	67·5
Stroke	115	110	110
cc capacity	2443	3150	2356
Valves	sleeve	sleeve	sleeve
BHP			
Maker's rating	16·8	22·6	16·7
Carburation	Zenith	Zenith	Cozette/ s/charge
Cooling System	Pump	Pump	Pump
Lubrication System	Pressure	Pressure	Pressure
Gear box	4 Σ R	4 Σ R	4 Σ R
Rear axle ratio	4·2:1	4·5:1	4·17:1
Transmission	Torque Tubel Spiral Bevel	Torque Tube Spiral Bevel	Torque Tube Spiral Bevel
Suspension F/R	½e cant.	½e cant.	½e cant.
Wheel base length	10'7½"	11'3"	10'7½"
Track width	4'8½"	4'8½"	4'8½"
Weight (cwt)	28		
Tyre size: front	31x5.26	33x6	31x5.26
Tyre size: rear			
Wheels	Wire	Wire	Wire
Price (£): chassis	498	698	573*
Price (£): complete	598	798	673

*In unsupercharged form the price was £75 less

BEARDMORE MOTOR COMPANY: THE BEARDMORE TAXI

Beardmore Motor Company – taxis and commercial vehicles

BEARDMORE Motor Company first exhibited at the Olympia Show in 1919 with three models. The first was a SV four-cylinder 1656cc with a two-seater body and dickey seat, manufactured at the Anniesland factory. The second was a four-cylinder side-valve 2413cc and was the taxi chassis made in Paisley. The third was from the Coatbridge factory, a four-cylinder side-valve 4072cc. This was displayed with a chauffeur-driven saloon body. As far as this can be proven, G. W. A. Brown was responsible for all these engines.

To provide work for the Paisley factory in 1913 when Arrol-Johnston moved to Heathhall, Beardmore experimented with the American-designed

1919 Beardmore Taxi Mk I.

electrically-driven coupé made by the Detroit Electric Company under licence from Edison Accumulators Ltd. Arrol-Johnston contracted to build 50 cars, and at least one was built. It successfully travelled 380 miles from Dumfries to London, leaving on a Monday morning (9 June 1913) and arriving in London on the Wednesday morning (11 June). The weight of the car with driver and passenger was 57cwt. The 60-cell battery weighed 900lbs and the single series wound motor was rated at 3½hp with a reduction gear of 6:1. The speed on the level was 18mph.

This interest in electric vehicles probably stemmed from Arrol-Johnston's earlier experiments with Blackwood Murray's design. The problem of what to do with the Paisley factory was solved by the outbreak of war and they turned over to munitions, manufacturing 18-pounder field guns and shells. However, the electric coupé had sown the seeds of a future development.

The end of the war left Beardmore with several empty factories and several possible products with which to fill them. One of these products was a four-cylinder side-valve engine designed for the Ministry of Munitions. It was intended to start engines on airships by means of a two-pronged shaft which fitted over the boss of the propeller, the whole being mounted on a mobile chassis and known as a Hucks starter. The origin of this engine was without doubt the 15.9 Arrol-Johnston. However, Brown's redesign was sufficiently extensive for it to be regarded as completely new. The work included new monoblock cylinders, detachable head and a new crankcase, with the magneto and tandem generator (when fitted) driven by Morse chains at the front of the engine. A Bell Housing incorporated the gearbox in unit construction. Only the crankshaft, con rods and pistons remained the same.

The planning for the Beardmore taxi started in 1915. No doubt it had been quickly realised that the electric car intended for the Paisley factory

1919 Beardmore Taxi Mk I chassis.

was not a practical proposition, but the basic idea for a short-haul city vehicle had been born. A new company was floated. The chief draughtsman was E. Baird; B. J. Angus-Shaw, who had designed the successful side-valve Sunbeams in 1904, was general manager; and A. McMurray was in charge of testing and development. A design was laid down to meet the requirements of Scotland Yard who, at that time, had jurisdiction over the type of vehicle allowed to be used as a taxi cab. In fact these regulations were ridiculously out-of-date and restrictive, thereby adding considerably to the cost of the vehicle. For example, they were still insisting on oil lamps well into the 1920s, and when electricity was finally permitted a standby oil rear lamp was called for.

The aero starter engine was rated at 15.6hp 2.4 litres and had the highly desirable characteristic of high torque at low speed 32bhp at 2000 rev/min. (It may have been that this engine was also designed as a replacement for the out-of-date 15.9 Arrol-Johnston and rejected by Pullinger.) When production got underway in 1919 it proved to be an immediate success, setting the standard for taxi cab design in large cities for many years. The Beardmore taxi was referred to as the 'Rolls-Royce' of cabs and the complete cab, bodywork, trim, *etc* was originally produced entirely in Scotland. Another secret of its success was a favourable hire purchase scheme. In those days many of London's taxi cabs were owned by the individual drivers, while the 'Coupé Company' owned 2000, with a staff of 80 mechanics to look after them. A service depot was later established in North London and eventually the complete production of taxis was transferred there in order to be near the main market. By 1928 over 6000 taxis had been made at the Paisley factory.

The Beardmore Mark I was no adaptation – it was designed solely for the job. The chassis was in-swept at the front to allow the minimum turning circle of 25 feet on full lock and the side members were down-swept between the front and rear wheels. This enabled the body rockers to be left full strength at the doors and at the same time lowered the height of the door sill for easy entry and exit. The engine was mounted in a sub frame at an angle of two and a half degrees so that when loaded the propeller shaft was in a straight line from the gearbox to the rear axle. The flexible couplings were Hardy disc pattern. The wheel base was eight feet one inch, which accommodated a roomy compartment capable of seating five people.

In addition to the manufacture of taxi cabs, the Paisley company also produced commercial vehicles. There was a 30cwt truck chassis employing the 2.4 litre engine, along with a Ferodo-lined cone clutch and four-speed gearbox having ratios of 28.8, 16.45, 11.52 and 7.2:1. A charabanc chassis was also produced with a higher rear axle ratio giving a 6.4:1 in top gear. The rear axle was the fully-floating type with worm drive. The rear wheel brakes were

15 x 2¼ inches internal expanding type, tyres were 820 x 120 twins on rear or single 895 x 135 all round, and the electrics were six volt. The chassis was rugged, well proven and priced at £395. Bodies for either type were available. The 'Dundee' van cost £495 and the 16-seater 'Paisley' coach was £675. When the Anniesland light car factory ceased production in 1926, the assembly of the Mark III taxi was transferred from Paisley to Anniesland. The taxi engine was also used to power two new models: the Beardmore 'Stewart' saloon and the Beardmore chauffeur-driven landaulette. Parts for about 250 of these cars were ordered, but again they proved to be loss-makers and were discontinued in 1927. These two models are dealt with under the 'light car' details (discussed later).

Financial viability was always a problem. The Paisley works made a net loss of £97,793 between 1920 and 1925, although the last three years had been profitable. Based on these results, in 1925 the company managed to obtain Treasury guarantees from the Trade Facilities Act Advisory Committee for a loan of £350,000 to fund their taxi hire purchase schemes. It was a condition of the loan that the Paisley works be hived off to form a separate company, Beardmore (Paisley) Ltd, with a capital of £250,000, and that a separate selling company, Beardmore Taxicabs Ltd, be formed. Beardmore (Paisley) Ltd was to rent the Paisley works from the parent company for £3000 per year. The Treasury had the right to nominate a director to the boards of both Beardmore Taxicabs Ltd and Beardmore Motor Company.

Despite assistance under the Trade Facilities Acts, Beardmore (Paisley) Ltd and the Van Street commercial vehicle works, Beardmore Taxicabs Ltd and Beardmore Motor Company remained unprofitable. From 1925-30 Beardmore (Paisley) Ltd made a net loss of £78,506, mainly due to an unsuccessful foray into van production in 1926.

In 1931 Captain Irving was again called in to act as consultant to the three firms. Taking his advice Beardmore (Paisley) Ltd tried to reach agreement with Beardmore Taxicabs on a revised sales price for a redesigned vehicle. Beardmore Taxicabs refused to allow an increase and in 1932 the taxi-manufacturing business was sold to Beardmore Motor Company. This company acquired the old engine works at Grove Park, Hendon, previously owned by Aster Engineering and rented by Beardmore Motor Company since 1922.

William Beardmore & Company Ltd formed a separate commercial vehicle department in 1929 to manage the Van Street works and to acquire the manufacturing rights of the successful French eight-wheeler Chenard-Walcker heavy haulage tractor and trailer (see page 88). In 1932 the entire taxi cab manufacture was transferred to Hendon over a period of time. In 1932 there were Paisley-built cabs, Hendon-built cabs with Beardmore engines, and also Hendon-built cabs with Commer engines. The aero engine company, now concentrating on diesel engines, moved into the Paisley

Make	BEARDMORE TAXI				
Year	1919-24	1924-29	hyper 1929-33	1934-35	1936-37
Model	Mk I	Mk II	Mk III	Mk IV	Mk V
Factory	Paisley		Anniesland	Hendon	Hendon
Nº CYL	4	4	4	4	4
Bore	80	80	72	72/75	commer 75
Stroke	120	120	120	120/110	110
cc capacity	2409	2409	1954	1954/1944	1944
Valves	S.V.	S.V.	S.V. Ricardo	S.V.	S.V.
BHP	32 @ 2000	24 @ 1500		48 @ 3800	48 @ 3800
Maker's rating	15·6	15·6	12·8	13·9	13·9
Carburation	Zenith	Zenith F	Zenith F	Zenith H F Solex 30	Solex 30
Cooling system	T.S.	T.S.	T.S.	T.S.	Pump
Lubrication system	Forced	Forced	Forced	Forced	Forced
Gear box	4 Σ R	4 Σ R	4 Σ R	4 Σ R	4 Σ R
Rear axle ratio	7·2:1	7·2:1	5·5:1	5·5:1	5·4:1
Transmission	Bevel	Spiral Bevel	Spiral Bevel	Worm	Worm
Suspension F/R	½e ¾e	½e ¾e	½e ¾e	½e ¾e	½e ½e
Wheel base length	8'6"	8'6"	9'	9'6"	9'6"
Track width	4'6"	4'6"	4'7"	4'8"	4'8"
Weight (cwt)	18	18	18	19	19
Tyre size: front	815x105	815x105	30x5"	20x5	30x5
Tyre size: rear					
Wheels	wood spoke	steel spoke	steel spoke	disc	disc
Price (£): chassis	450	395	365		
Price (£): complete	650				

1937-39	1946-53	1954-58	1958-64	1958-64	1964-67	1965-68
Mk VI	oxford I II III	Mk VII	Mk VII	Mk VII diesel	Mk VII	Mk VIII
Hendon Paisley						
4	4	4	4	4	4	
75	wolseley 75	consul 79·37	consul 204E 82·55	perking 76.20	zephyr 211E 82.55	
110	102	76·2	79·50	88·9	79·50	
1944	1802	1508	1703	1621	1703	
S.V.	OHV	OHV	OHV	OHV	OHV	
48 @ 3800		47 @ 4400	59 @ 4400	43 @ 4600	68 @ 4800	
13·9						
Zenith 30 vec	S U	Zenith 34 vn	Zenith 34 vn	Fuel injection	Zenith	
Pump	Pump	Pump	Pump	Pump	Pump	
Forced	Forced dry sump	Forced	Forced	Forced	Forced	
4 Σ R	4 Σ R	3 Σ R	3 Σ R	3 Σ R	3 Σ R	
5·4:1	5·166:1	5·875:1	5·875:1	5·875:1	5·875:1	
Worm	Spiral Bevel	Hypoid	Hypoid	Hypoid	Hypoid	
½e ½e	½e ½e	½e ½e	½e ½e	½e ½e	½e ½e	
9'6"	8'11½"	8'8"	8'8"	8'8"	8'8"	
4'8"	4'8 5/16"	4'8¾"	4'8¾"	4'8¾"	4'8¾"	
19			28	28	28	
20x5	550x18	5·75x16	5·75x16	5·75x16	5·75x16	
disc	disc	disc	disc	disc	disc	

Metro Cab by M C W based on designs by M C W/Beardmore after the winding up of Beardmore Taxi Co.

Borgward diesel engines available for Mk II and Mk III

Left: one of the last Paisley-built taxis; right: sectioned engine 1919.

Linwood factory. The cab bodies for the Hendon-produced taxis were built by Weymann at their Addlestone works. This state of affairs continued until 1939. After World War II there was an agreement with the Nuffield organisation, the cabs being made by Wolseley. Under this regime the 'Oxford' cab was produced and actually used a bored-out MG cylinder block (1802cc) push-rod OHV complete with dry sump lubrication.

Beardmore resumed the manufacture of taxis from early 1955. Ford 'Consul' (and later four-cylinder 'Zephyr') engines were used, as well as Perkins Diesels. The last 'Zephyr' engine cab was built in 1967. The various models were as follows: the Mark I (1919) was in production until 1923 and was withdrawn from service in 1933; the Mark II was in production until 1926, coming out of service in 1936; the Mark III hyper, known for some obscure reason to the trade as the 'farthing cab', ceased production in 1932 and was withdrawn from service in 1946; the 'Oxford', the first OHV London Taxi Marks I, II and III lasted from 1947–53, but you could still ride in an MG-engined Beardmore until 1963.

An attempt to sell the company to Daimler failed and by 1969 the company had lost much of its business to Austin.

The designs were sold to Metro Cammel Weyman and the new MCW cabs originally showed their Beardmore origins. Today MCW cabs are much in evidence on the streets of London. The factory at Hendon became Henley's (a large car agency) service station. It would be interesting to know if any of the 6000 cabs built between 1919 and 1928 have survived. Surely this famous vehicle deserves to be preserved. The London Vintage Taxi Association has examples of Marks III, IV, V, VI and VII owned by members of the association.

TEMPLE WORKS:
THE ANNIESLAND BEARDMORE

**Temple Works – the Anniesland light car –
the ill-fated aluminium side-valve engine – the taxi-engined cars**

FOR the sporting enthusiast the Beardmore light car was the highlight of his enterprises. During the war the company's activities were spread over a vast product range, among them the manufacture of diesel engines for tanks. One such engine was a 400hp unit for the Mark V heavy tank which required a donkey engine to start it. This may have been the origin of either the light-weight OHC four-cylinder 1487cc engine or the side-valve 1656cc. There can be no doubt that Beardmore had an eye for the future and the fact that these engines were eminently suitable for installation in a car chassis was no coincidence. The OHC engine had two main bearings and produced 26bhp at 3000 rev/min, being rated at 10.5hp. The engine had inclined valves operated by an overhead camshaft driven by skew gears. This immediately

1919 Beardmore 10/18 model light car. J H Hurst driving.

recalls the 1908 Beeston Humber which had a similar camshaft drive, as had the ill-fated 'Victory' engine. The designer was undoubtedly G. W. A. Brown. Unfortunately, in this case, the engine had an inherent design fault in the skew gear drive to the overhead camshaft. Skew gear drive for overhead camshafts was fairly common. Bugatti and Napier employed them, but due to the limitations of this type of gear they were soon discarded in favour of spiral bevels or chains. The OHC Beardmore light car was thus launched with an engine that was apparently satisfactory. The fact that it chewed up its camshaft gears was only discovered once it was in production.

The car first saw the light of day in 1919 and the intention was to use the 1487cc OHC unit. However, for the purpose of the show, the side-valve 1656cc engine was fitted. There seems to have been some duplication of intent between Anniesland and Tongland. The Beardmore preceded the Tongland-built Galloway by a year. The Galloway design had nothing to do with Beardmore, except that his company had links with Fiat. Perhaps the difference between the dull Galloway and the potentially spritely OHC Beardmore sums up the basic differences between Beardmore and Pullinger – Pullinger was restricted by rigid dogmatism, while Beardmore was totally unrestricted, even by finance. Only this can explain the logic of starting up a new car company while already owning one which could have done the same thing.

My father purchased one of the first Beardmore cars to be built. It had been used as a demonstration model and he naturally got it very cheaply (£40). It was not a bad car – a two-seater, similar to the show model with a dickey seat. The specification was a bit bleak: there was no electric starter, it had two wheel brakes, there was no windscreen wiper (a sliced potato was supposed to keep the screen clear), it had minimum instrumentation, while the headlamps and radiator, *etc* were made of unplated brass. Inevitably my father had to have the timing gears replaced, which was hardly a plus for reliability. They always announced their impending departure by a clattering sound that gradually grew in intensity as the need for replacement became more urgent.

Another weakness was the use of Oldham-type universal joints on the drive shaft. Contained in leather gaiters which neither retained the lubrication nor excluded dirt, the result was more clanking sounds.

The OHC car was committed to production, but with no reliable engine to use, a stop-gap had to be found. Two side-valve models were listed for the 1920 season: a 1656cc and, obviously, the taxi engine. Not many, if any, of the small side-valve cars were built. The prolonged foundry moulders' strike of 1920 may have been a blessing in disguise, providing an enforced respite during which the company could sort out its problems.

The 1920-21 season saw the return of the OHC engine with modifications to the camshaft drive but still using skew gears; the bore and stroke was increased to that of the smaller side-valve unit. The Anniesland factory was now fully equipped for engine production. There was a large plano-miller for cylinder blocks, gear cutting machines, gear grinders, *etc*, so they were independent of Paisley.

The revised OHC engine incorporated a type of ratchet-operated one-way brake on the camshaft which damped out oscillations from the skew gears – a similar device was also used on the Napier. This device did not cure the defect but merely postponed the onset of the clattering sound.

During this period George Allsworth and Francis M. Luther reappeared as directors of the company. They were still agents for Austro Daimler. The two other directors were William Beardmore and J. A. Girdwood (Beardmore company secretary).

Allsworth and Luther operated a company named Aidee Ltd, registered as makers and dealers in motorcars, carriages, vehicles, boats and aero engines. Beardmore purchased Aidee Ltd, thus becoming the agent for Austro Daimler cars, and there seems to have been no directors at Anniesland from Beardmore (Paisley) Ltd. Luther was appointed managing director of the new company. A DOHC Austro Daimler 1.5 litre racing car was used as a guinea pig by the experimental department, and on occasion chief engineer Alf Francis gave me a rapid 'round the houses' run in it. (No details of Francis' background are available, but it is probable that he was a motorcycle man who was acquired when Beardmore took over Frank E. Baker's Precision company, an episode covered later in this story, see page 82). How much the design of the Beardmore was influenced by Austro Daimler is uncertain, since the engine design remained faithful to Brown's original plans. Luther continued to represent Austro Daimler and imported the 1.5 litre DOHC cars via the former Aster but now Beardmore depot at Hendon. One must therefore conclude that Austro Daimler condoned Luther's association with the Beardmore light car, even though it was in competition with their own product to some extent.

The Beardmore was not a cheap car and, as produced in Scotland, tended to be a bit heavy. The 1656cc car lasted until 1923, during which time the skew gear drive was dropped in favour of Morse chain. Due mainly to the insistence of the sales staff and distributors, and perhaps as an excuse for failing to reach their sales targets, the engine size seems to have been increased rather frequently – in 1923 the car became 1857cc.

The model was called the 11.9. The sports version used magnesium alloy pistons among other innovations. It would seem that this engine was still based on the original 1920 design as far as the cylinder head was concerned. The engine was bored out to 74mm in 1924 giving it a capacity of 1962cc. Cyril Paul, Beardmore's test driver, broke the record at the Shelsley Walsh 1924

Above: Beardmore tourer
12/30; right: engine.
(Photographs courtesy of Graham Thomas)

meeting with a time of 50.5 seconds, beating Raymond May's Bugatti and Humphrey Cook's Vauxhall. The block was bored out to 74.5mm giving a capacity of 1988cc; it also recorded a speed of 109mph at Brooklands. This car and the 12/30 are said to have been redesigned by Alf Francis, but the change in the method of driving the camshaft seems to have been the only major modification. On the 12/30 the bore was reduced to 72.5mm 1854cc, probably because the wall thickness of the cylinders gave rise to porosity and left no room for re-bores. The two-litre engine was a logical development of Brown's original design, which had now been stretched to its limit. The two-bearing crankshaft was the Achilles' heel of these later engines – plans for a three main bearing crankshaft had been in existence for some time but were never given the go ahead.

In 1923 the 1656cc car in two-seater form sold for £475; the four-seater tourer was £495. The short wheelbase sports model cost £550; the 1960cc Shelsley Walsh car with sports body cost £650. The weight was about 16.5cwt and the rear axle ratio 4.15:1. It is reported that Sir Henry Birkin bought one for his girlfriend who had the car painted pale violet, much to his disgust.

Above: 1924 Beardmore sportscar
12/30; left: engine.
(Photographs courtesy of Mr David McIvor)

Beardmore did not enter races but ran a steady campaign of hill climbs, speed tests and trials, building up a very good reputation in the process.

After car number one, my father purchased one of the new 1.6 litre cars, which was vastly superior to the original car and would do an easy 60mph in four-seater form with the screen up. This car was regrettably abandoned in favour of the Arrol-Johnston already mentioned, but my father went back to Beardmore again with an 1857cc car.

In 1924 there was a big reorganisation at the Anniesland works. The Paisley management took over and the entire marketing policy of the company was reversed. It appears that Alf Francis departed some time in 1925 and with him went any hope of the rumoured 2.3 litre three main-bearing OHC engine. As for Cyril Paul, the test driver, the new models were of a very pedestrian nature and his services could be of no further value.

In October 1924 the company introduced two new engines which were both four-cylinder and approximately the same size. This seemed a very odd thing to do. The first model was called the 14/40 and was a side-valve unit

67

with a cast aluminium block and pressed-in cast iron liners. The magneto was driven from a cross-shaft by skew gears from the camshaft at the front of the engine whilst the dynamo was driven in the same manner from the camshaft at the rear of the engine, on the opposite side from the magneto. The exhaust manifold was swept well forward, presumably to avoid cooking the insulation of the dynamo wires. The capacity was 2298cc.

It was intended that this car would be produced at the Anniesland works and it is probable that the engine was the work of Baird, chief draughtsman, and Angus-Shaw, general manager of the Paisley factory. Quite what they hoped to achieve is in some doubt. The design was expensive to produce and offered nothing in the way of improved performance. In fact, in their publicity brochures they went out of their way to explain that it was not a sports car, and furthermore that overhead valves were just a fad. They added that the increased efficiency was not important and that side-valve engines produced sufficient power for the purpose. All this was not without some humour. Arrol-Johnston, who adopted OHV shortly afterwards, was at pains to point out the great advantage over side-valve engines, proclaiming that OHV engines were the power units of the future.

The Beardmore claims did not, however, ring true because they fitted a large metal pressing on top of the cylinder head which enclosed the spark plugs and HT leads and gave the engine the appearance of an OHV. The chassis price was £425 and a five-seater touring body raised it to £560. The second car was intended for production at Paisley and was called the 16/40 and later the 16/60. This was a straightforward adaptation of the cast-iron taxi engine. The positioning of the gearbox was different however, not being unit construction, and it was carried on separate cross-chassis members. It also had a right-hand change gear lever. The chassis price was £375, and with a touring body £495.

The 12/30 OHC 1883cc car was continued without change: the chassis price was £295 and a four-seater touring body raised the price to £395. Not surprisingly the 14/40 was a non-seller and had been discontinued by the end of 1925. What possessed the company to make it in the first place remains a mystery. Angus-Shaw may have hoped to repeat his earlier successes with the SV Sunbeams and perhaps it is this engine which has been mistaken for the long-awaited 2.3 litre OHC engine with three main-bearings. Certainly the bogus 'valve cover' on top of the SV head may have misled some, and the engine as shown at Olympia in 1924 looked most impressive, with an aluminium tray completely fitting between the crankcase and chassis side members. The entire engine had been polished and given a machine-turned finish, and the aluminium plates covering the core spaces for the water jackets were attached by a large number of small diameter nuts and studs reminiscent of aircraft practice. However, one is still left wondering what the point was. The company was in serious financial trouble and the last thing it needed was the high development costs that such an unorthodox engine would incur.

The urgent need was for the development of a three main-bearing crankshaft for the 12/30. This would have opened the way for further development of this highly successful OHC engine. The decision to go for the all-aluminium 14/40 bears the hallmarks of Beardmore himself: a disregard for financial implications, a fascination with mechanical curiosities, and 'last ditch' defiance in the face of bankruptcy. Later, the four-valve OHC Beardmore 'Precision' motorcycle engine and the sleeve-valve supercharged Arrol-Aster all had considerable technical merit and helped to keep their companies afloat. The 14/40 engine, on the other hand, was just a very expensive blunt instrument, and there is no doubt that this aberration was one of the factors which led to the demise of the company.

It had been a despairing attempt to keep the Anniesland factory alive, but like so many of Beardmore's projects it was never thought through and there had been insufficient testing done on a prototype. The designers appeared to think that because the engine had been successful in cast iron, it would be equally so in aluminium. However, the main castings distorted under heat and load, and cylinder head gasket problems and valve seats which worked loose were but a few of the 'unexpected' snags. In addition there was no logic in spending money on a lightweight engine and then installing it in a chassis with heavy bodywork.

My father had been considering buying one of the new 2.3 litre cars. However, one day we were walking along the main road which led to Anniesland when a 2.3 litre test chassis passed us. My father knew the driver and he stopped for a chat. Asked if he should buy one, my father's friend replied to the effect that he would not touch it with a barge pole. Most of the motoring public agreed with that opinion. The Paisley car was continued until 1928 and the 16/40 was called the 'Colonial' model and sold as a five-seater open tourer and a saloon that resembled a slightly-enlarged taxi. The company advertised it as a motor carriage for family men of moderate means. Since the driver's compartment was open to the elements and divided from the rear by a glass partition, it would have suited the family man with a large noisy family.

The 16/60 carried virtually the same bodywork as the 16/40. Both were specified as seven-seaters and available with the front compartment open to the elements (the 'Stewart') and as a saloon with the rear part of the body able to be folded open (the 'Lomond' ¾ landaulette). The company brochure described the appearance as 'dignified'! Parts for about 250 vehicles were ordered, but nothing like that quantity was built. The scheme was abandoned in 1928, having cost the company about £40,000.

Cyril Paul breaking the record at Shelsley Walsh. (Demaus Transport Photographics)

The Beardmore car was in direct competition with such makes as Alvis, Aston Martin, Riley, Lea Francis and a host of other sporting vehicles, but its weight and high price made it uncompetitive in a crowded market. Beardmore, via J. H. Kelly & Company, built their own bodywork and had such things as sliding seats with adjustable rake. The cushions were nine inches deep, built up from two layers of springs, and were covered with the best quality cow hide, diamond pleated and buttoned. There were footrests for the rear passengers and the whole car was of the highest quality. Unfortunately, all these refinements and limited production pushed up costs and with the abandonment of the OHC engine it lost its place in the market without offering an acceptable alternative.

Another endemic problem, and one that haunted the entire organisation, seemed to be that engines were never ready on time. Beardmore frequently exhibited their cars at the Scottish Motor Show at Kelvin Hall with locked bonnets and strapped-up front springs, as no engines were available in time for the show. By 1928 all production had ceased, the company having lost £96,012 between 1922 and 1926.

THE COATBRIDGE
BEARDMORE

The Coatbridge Beardmore – description of engine and experiments with pneumatic suspension

THE Coatbridge factory began as the British wing of an American firm. In the late 1880s, for some strange reason, the W. K. V. Lidgerwood Corporation of the United States of America decided to open a marine engine manufacturing company at Coatbridge. Lidgerwood was better known in America as the builder of self-propelled steam winches for logging. The marine steam engine followed British practice and employed the Beardmore-Fiat Caprotti poppet-valve gear. Engines up to 1000hp were produced under the marque of Speedwell.

During World War I Lidgerwood seems to have been controlled by Beardmore and to have been purchased outright by the company in 1915. As previously related it was the centre of an attempt to continue the manufacture of aero engines at the factory which had been one of the main suppliers of the 160hp engines. Beardmore also had a contract for the manufacture of ABC engines through his association with Vickers. Vickers recognised a dud when it saw one and quickly passed the contract to the unsuspecting Beardmore.

Beardmore also attempted to buy back as many 160hp engines as he could lay his hands on. Unfortunately the government sold these engines as scrap, which entailed hitting them with a sledgehammer. A truckload of such engines cost £15. Even if the engines had been able to be repaired, they were already dated, and in any case there were no buyers. It was the same with the 'BHP'. Siddeley had removed the ground from under its feet. Not only was it less developed than the 'Puma', it was no longer interchangeable. The Beardmore Aero Engine Company at Dalmuir seemed to have had nothing to do with this Coatbridge project.

Plans to build aeroplanes and install Beardmore engines were no more realistic (aircraft built by Beardmore during the war are discussed on page 89).

As a matter of interest a 160hp Beardmore aero engine, rebuilt at Coatbridge and running at 700 rev/min, was employed to drive a generator to supply power to the King's Norton factory of Beardmore 'Precision'. At the same time and, again apparently without any assessment of probable demand, another venture was launched – the production of the Beardmore 30hp car, making use of a four-cylinder 4072cc side-valve engine already in existence.

Beardmore undoubtedly liked large cars, although the origins of the 4072cc four-cylinder side-valve engine are unknown. There are unconfirmed scraps of information which suggest that Beardmore built at least one armoured car. They were certainly involved in the production of armour plate for these vehicles and Leyland built some using plate which had been cut and prepared by Beardmore for assembly at Leyland. Other manufacturers such as Talbot and Lanchester sent their chassis out to have the armour-plated shell fitted. There is no record of where they went, but it could well have been Beardmore who supplied pressed-steel chassis members for armoured cars. Again there is no record of who the customers were. T. M. Service of Beardmore had developed a technique for curving armour plate for rotating gun turrets, *etc* and Beardmore had the necessary machinery and skills for this class of work. They also built about 50 Mark IV tanks and unspecified number of Marks Vs.

The four-litre engine was most probably designed by Brown and features of the design suggest that it was for applications where the airflow around the sump was restricted. It is impossible to say whether it was intended for an armoured car, or as a portable electric generator set, or possibly for marine use. It was probably used to power lifeboats and ships' pinnaces which Beardmore constructed as part of the equipment supplied to the battleships built at the Dalmuir shipyards. Parts for 250 vehicles were ordered, but there is some doubt as to how many were actually built – estimates vary from two to 15 to 30 (this latter figure comes from George Allsworth, director with Francis M. Luther of the Austro Daimler UK agency, and is probably the correct one). Photographs of two open four-seater tourers and a saloon exist, and the writer saw a large *coupé de ville* in the paint shop of J. H. Kelly & Company, the coachwork builders who supplied the taxi and some light car bodies. It was finished in dark green but did not have the Beardmore trademark of the sloping filler cap.

Making enquiries, I was told that this car was designed to compete with the Rolls-Royce. It is unlikely, however, that this announcement caused concern at Derby. Rather it was typical of the Beardmore approach to market research: having a four-litre engine available, the company decided to build a car and then see if it would sell. Large capacity four-cylinder cars were common, but the quality market demanded much more refinement. Unfortunately there was nothing about the car that could not have been produced just as well, if not better, by Arrol-Johnston. Pullinger-permitting, this venture cost £259,000 and lasted little more than two years. Although the engines were produced at Coatbridge, the cars were probably assembled at Linwood. It is unlikely this vast amount of money was lost solely on the cars. It was probably a combination of the overall cost of the car and a vain attempt to re-establish aero engine manufacture. Nonetheless, it was another example of a loss-making venture whose viability had been fully researched in the first place.

The designer of the 30hp car was Henry Elvidge AMIAE. Elvidge had worked for Napier, Rolls-Royce, BSA, Austin, Siddeley-Deasy, and of course Humber. At the time of his appointment he was head draughtsman in the engine drawing office of the Royal Aircraft Establishment at Farnborough. Without doubt, his real purpose at Coatbridge was concerned with the aero engines.

The manager of the Coatbridge car department was J. Beattie, who was formerly works manager at Vulcan and had also worked for Argyll and Crossley. Beattie was also manager of the aero engine department, and the marine diesel engine and centrifugal pump departments. He also shared management of the marine steam engine department with J. M. McKenzie.

The cars were nominally Beardmore Motor Company, but had different directors, management and factory. The aero engines were nominally Beardmore Aero Engine Company, but the same applied to them as the cars. The marine steam and diesel engine was nominally William Beardmore Company Dalmuir. If there was ever a recipe for disaster, this was it. The 30hp chassis was conventional enough, the suspension was by half elliptics all round and a torque tube anchored to a cross member at the rear of the gearbox, which was a separate unit and controlled the movement of the rear axle. An external contracting transmission brake was hand-operated, while the internal expanding shoes of the rear wheel brakes were operated by the brake pedal.

A Ferodo-lined cone clutch, four-speed gearbox and spiral bevel rear axle completed the design which incorporated Rudge Whitworth wire spoke wheels. The four-cylinder engine was basically conventional and was claimed to be exceptionally smooth and quiet. The monoblock cylinder casting was bolted to an aluminium crankcase which was attached to the chassis by four arms. The Zenith carburettor was on the opposite side from the exhaust manifold and fed the cylinders via a manifold cast in the block.

The magneto and water pump were driven by skew gears from a cross-shaft at the front of the engine and a cast aluminium fan was driven by a whittle belt. The dynamo, which was not required originally, was mounted on the scuttle and driven by a further whittle belt from a pulley on the rear of the camshaft. If the drives to the auxiliaries sound complicated, then the lubrication system was even more so. An aluminium tank with an oil level gauge was mounted at the rear of the engine on a cross member which largely shielded it from the air flow, so cooling of the oil did not appear to be a primary consideration. A skew gear on the camshaft drove no less than three oil pumps in tandem. The main pump drew oil from the aluminium reservoir and delivered it under pressure to the crankshaft bearings; the second pump drew oil from the reservoir and fed it to the camshaft bearings; whilst the third pump scavenged the sump returning the oil to the reservoir. This system was usually applied to very much more sophisticated designs where the oil reservoir provided cooling to the lubricating oil, but in this application it is difficult to

Make	BEARDMORE					
Year	1919	1919-21	1921-22	1920-23	1922-23	1924-2
Model	10/18	11·9	11·9	15/20	12·30	12/30
Factory	Anniesland					
Nº CYL	4	4	4	4	4	4
Bore	65	68	68	80	72-74	74/74
Stroke	112	114	114	120	114	114
cc capacity	1487	1656	1656	2413	1860/1960	1960/19
Valves	OHC	S.V.	OHC	S.V.	OHC	OHC
BHP	26 @ 2500		26 @ 2500	20.5 @ 1500 30 @ 3000	26 @ 2000 30 @ 3000	70
Maker's rating	9·8	10·8	11·5	15·9	11.5/12·8	12.8/13
Carburation	Zenith	Zenith	Zenith	Zenith	Claudel	Zenith
Cooling system	T.S.	T.S.	T.S.	Pump	T.S.	T.S.
Lubrication system	Forced	Forced	Forced	Forced	Forced	Forced
Gear box	4 Σ R	3 Σ R	4 Σ R**	4 Σ R	4 Σ R	4 Σ R
Rear axle ratio		4·5:1	4·5:1	4·5:1	4·5:1/4·15:1	4·15:1
Transmission	Spiral Bevel	Spiral Bevel	Spiral Bevel	Spiral Bevel	Spiral Bevel	Spiral Be
Suspension F/R	½e ½e	½e ½e	½e ½e	½e ½e	½e ½e	½e ½
Wheel base length	8'6"	9'6"	8'9"	10'6"	9'6"	9'6"/8'6
Track width	4'2"	4'2"	4'2"	4'6"	4'2"	4'2"
Weight (cwt)			11	19		16½
Tyre size: front	710x90	760x90	760x90	815x105	760x90	30x3½
Tyre size: rear						
Wheels	Artillery	Artillery	Artillery	Artillery	Artillery	Artillery/M
Price: chassis					475 495 sports	
Price: complete			550	495	570 2 str 595 4 str	

650 sports
725 saloon and
Shelsley Walsh model

					BEARDMORE 30HP
1925-26	1925-26	1925-29	1926-29		1920-21
12/30	14/40	colonial 16/40	stewart 16/60		20/30
		Paisley			Coatbridge
4	4	4	4		4
72·5	75	80	80		90
114	130	120	130		160
1883	2298	2391	2614		4072
OHC	S.V.	S.V.	S.V.		S.V.
	37 @ 2600				50 @ 1600
12·8	13·9	15-16			30
Zenith	Zenith	Zenith	Zenith		Zenith
T.S.	Pump	Pump	Pump		T.S.
Forced	Forced	Forced	Forced		Forced
4 Σ R	4 Σ R	4 Σ R	4 Σ R		4 Σ R
4·9:1	4·5:1	4·28:1	4·28:1		3·43:1
Spiral Bevel	Spiral Bevel	Spiral Bevel	Spiral Bevel		Spiral Bevel
½e ½e	½e ½e	½e ½e	½e ½e		½e ½e
9'6"	10'3"	10'6"	12'9"		10'9"
4'2"	4'7"	4'7"	4'7"		4'6"
19					19
30x3½	765x105 775x105	820x120 33x6	820x120		820x120 895x135
Artillery/Wire	Artillery	Artillery	Artillery		Artillery/Wire
		315			
		445 495			

*Early batch 3 speed

see what possible advantage could have outweighed the complication and expense of the system. This reinforces the theory that these engines were originally designed for some purpose other than vehicle use. The 30hp car appeared briefly in the news once more in 1926 when a chassis with an open tourer body was used to demonstrate a pneumatic suspension system developed by the research department of the locomotive works at Dalmuir. The system provided a suspension which catered for variations of load and weight distribution and gave a level ride at constant height. The weight of the car was carried by four air cylinders, two per axle. Air at 100lb per square inch was supplied by a single-cylinder compressor via a reservoir and driven by a chain from the clutch shaft. The brakes were also pneumatically operated.

On the demonstration car the two main leafs of the front springs were retained in order to locate the axle. These exerted no influence on the pneumatic suspension and would have been replaced by radius arms on any future development. The air cylinders consisted of two tubular sections, one sliding inside the other. Multiple bucket seals sealed the space between the two sections and a small reservoir supplied lubricating oil to the sliding surfaces.

Inlet and outlet valves were arranged inside the inner cylinder so that they only came into operation if the normal up and down movement of the axle was exceeded. On ordinary road surfaces the vertical movement of the axle was accommodated by the compression of air within the cylinders. However, on extreme bumps the inlet valve opened allowing extra air into the cylinder and, on extreme rebounds, the exhaust valve allowed air to escape.

In a test the demonstration car was loaded unequally and then driven at 30mph over rough ground full of bumps and hollows. The car remained level with no pitching or rolling. It was claimed that under normal usage the compressor was only required to cut in about every 25 miles, and if the brakes were operated by other means then the distance went up to about 200 miles.

Unlike the Citroën, the chassis did not sink when the engine was switched off. The car could stand for several days without any alteration to the chassis level. The system was fully patented and appeared to offer great advantages, particularly in the luxury class of vehicle. However, no one took up the offer of manufacturing rights and one suspects that manufacturing costs and vulnerability to wear of the sliding seals were the main drawbacks.

Like so many of Beardmore's innovations it was ahead of its time, and ahead of current technology. Because of this the complications exceeded the advantages and nothing further was heard of it until Citroën perfected the idea with the aid of materials not available to Beardmore at that time.

The Coatbridge company was sold off when the Beardmore empire collapsed. It finally disappeared in 1939 when the factory was taken over by Martin Black & Company, manufacturers of wire ropes. The Speedwell factory at Coatbridge was finally closed down and demolished in 1970.

F. E. BAKER LTD AND THE BEARDMORE PRECISION MOTORCYCLE, KING'S NORTON, BIRMINGHAM

F. E. Baker Ltd – Beardmore Precision Motorcycle – Barr & Stroud – attempts to win the 350cc and 250cc TT races

TO try to make sense of Beardmore's management policy, if he ever had one, is impossible. Both Beardmore Motor Company and Beardmore Aero Engine Company consisted of a series of 'empires', none of which seemed to be on speaking terms with the others. All had their own designers and drawing offices, and all pursued different policies.

Arrol-Johnston, which was Pullinger's empire, should have been forced to use Brown's taxi engine with modifications to the bore and stroke. Anniesland's light car company could then have taken over the 'Victory' design which incorporated the three-bearing crankshaft which they so urgently needed; the fixtures, tools and patterns, along with a great many components, would also have been available to them.

The troubles experienced by Arrol-Johnston with the development of the 230hp engine* could have been solved by Beardmore Aero Engine Company, because they had access to Theo Biggs through their co-operation with Precision Engineering Company.

Biggs had already gained experience of the use of aluminium and in any case the engine had already been modified by Halford to incorporate Biggs'

---

* The 230hp engine eventually became the 250hp engine. Since no alterations were made to the bore or stroke, the extra 20hp must have been gained by improvements in design such as the three-valve head and the successful use of aluminium.

three-valve cylinder head design (Arrol-Johnston, as Biggs' former employer, owned the patents on the three-valve cylinder head). However, as already stated, they were all too busy building empires to have had time to talk to each other. The only liaison between these 'empires' was Beardmore himself. Worse was to follow when the Beardmore Aero Engine Company went into the motorcycle business, while Beardmore launched the Dunelt motorcycle (see page 84).

In 1919 the Beardmore Aero Engine Company, having supposedly worked closely with Frank E. Baker during the war, took a controlling interest in his Precision company. Co-operation between the two companies started very early on in the war. The King's Norton factory was taken over by the Ministry of Munitions and seems to have been fully occupied with work for Woolwich Arsenal. The real realm of co-operation appears to have been on the technical side. Baker, Biggs, and possibly S. J. H. Wilkes, formed a team of competent design engineers, but what role they played is unclear. Beardmore Aero Engine Company invested a great deal of money in them and they eventually became a subsidiary. The only official reason for this takeover was given as 'mutual interests', however, typical of the company's sloppy administration, Beardmore Aero Engine Company did not take over F. E. Baker Ltd and the name 'F. E. Baker' continued to appear on the engine plates of the Beardmore Precision motorcycle.

Baker had been apprenticed to the old Lovelace Cycle Works where he made friends with another apprentice, Theo Biggs. He worked first in America, then in England for the Eadie Manufacturing Company (makers of Royal Enfield cycles), and then as general manager of Premier Cycle Company. In 1906 he started a small factory in Birmingham with 20 employees. The original intention was to build up a business for the production of extremely accurate machine tools such as thread milling, jig boring machines and correcting lathes suitable for the production of jigs and gauges. However in 1910 he branched out into the production of motorcycle engines, one of his first being a 499cc side-valve unit designed by Wilkes. The Wilkes engine was very orthodox and similar to a dozen other units on the market. Nevertheless it was a great success and was swiftly followed by a whole range of engines, so that at the 1911 Olympia Show there were no less than 96 different models fitted with Baker's engines.

The demand was so great that the decision was taken to close down the other activities. The name 'Precision' was adopted and Frank Baker set about becoming the world's largest specialist manufacturer of motorcycle power units. In those days of frantic expansion, production was assisted by the Webley and Scott Company who manufactured components and even assembled some engines. This early success encouraged Baker to embark on a large works expansion programme which, because of unrealistic targets and overexpenditure, eventually landed the company in a serious financial crisis. Baker produced both two and four-stroke engines, 293cc, 499cc and 599cc side-valve single cylinder units, a 760cc SV Vee twin, and a 10hp water-cooled twin used by Montague Graham-White, a famous figure from the early days of flight, for his cycle car. Wilkes designed several successful engines for Precision, including the large Vee twins, which were used by several cycle car manufacturers including Warren Lambert, the 'Tiny' cycle car manufactured by Nanson Barker & Company, better known as manufacturers of the Airedale cars, the Sheffield Richardson, and the short-lived Merral Brown.

In 1912 Frank Baker made an arrangement with Gustavus Green to produce the Precision-Green engine which consisted of a Precision lower half with Green water-cooled cylinders using dimpled tank radiators mounted pannier-wise on the cylinder head. These engines fitted in Zenith frames had considerable success at Brooklands where they beat the 500cc one hour record and the 1000cc record, and they also broke all the side-car records up to two hours' duration.

The year 1913 saw the introduction of the Precision 'Junior' engine of 2hp 174cc. This interesting design incorporated a two-speed gear within the crankcase and also had horizontal valves operated by long levers from a camshaft in the crankcase. It was successful in competition and achieved the first climb up Mount Snowdon, reaching a height of 3500 feet. Calthorpe was also one of the many cycle makers who adopted this engine.

By 1914 the company was producing 100 engines per week and the number of employees had risen from 20 to 400. By 1918 manufacturing war material mainly for Woolwich Arsenal, the pay roll was over 800. Theo Biggs joined in 1913 as chief designer, having held a similar post at Raleigh, then Humber, and later Arrol-Johnston. Biggs designed the first Precision motorcycle, which was an advanced design with leaf-spring suspension at front and rear, the petrol tank consisting of two steel pressings welded together to form the top structural member of the frame. The mud-guards were rolled from heavy plate and also formed part of the suspension system.

However, before it came on the market in 1919 the Beardmore Aero Engine Company had obtained financial control and the bike became the Beardmore Precision. Several engine sizes were used: 348cc, 496cc and 598cc SV. This was in addition to the 350cc Barr & Stroud sleeve-valve engine which became standard wear as an alternative to Precision engines (Barr & Stroud also built motorcycles at their Anniesland factory).

It is said that the Beardmore Precision motorcycle was also built at the Anniesland car factory. It is possible that a few were assembled after the King's Norton factory closed. The Barr & Stroud company was just across the main road from the car factory and it seems as if they had very close ties with Beardmore. Barr & Stroud were famous for their optical instruments. During

World War I they made range finders, telescopic gun sights and gear for naval guns. And, as already mentioned, Beardmore built naval guns as well as battleships. It is interesting to note that in 1946, when the only Beardmore entity was still in existence, the Parkhead Forge – a consortium consisting of Beardmore, Barr & Stroud, Harland and Wolff Ltd, and ICI – was proposed for the purpose of supplying guns, mountings, explosives, propellants and fire control to British and foreign governments. Nothing, however, came of this initiative.

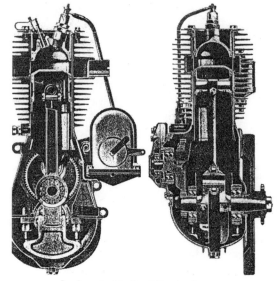

Beardmore Precision Barr & Stroud engine.
H. Ricondo, *The Internal Combustion Engine.*

As usual under the chairmanship of William Beardmore, Precision had an impressive competition programme with an equally impressive list of gold and silver cups and medals. In 1921 the company offered a 350cc two-stroke with cantilever spring frame, and a two-speed gearbox was incorporated in the engine unit. Gear ratios were 5:1 and 9:1, which at 2000 rev/min gave speeds of 28mph and 16mph. For use with a side-car, the ratios were 6.25:1 and 11.25:1 giving speeds of 24 and 13.5mph.

The gear change was effected by means of expanding clutches, each being driven by independent chains from the crankshaft and connecting by a final single chain to the rear wheel. The price solo was £95 and complete with side-car £105. It was claimed to be the first mass produced side-car unit ever offered to the market in Great Britain.

In 1922 the company offered a 'Sports Solo' which consisted of the 350cc two-stroke engine in a 'rigid' frame, *ie* without the cantilever springing and a two-speed Sturmey Archer gearbox in place of the enclosed twin chain unit. The price was £75. For an extra £10 the Barr & Stroud sleeve-valve engine could be fitted, and an additional £5 obtained a three-speed gearbox.

A new 4½hp four-stroke unit was also available with 598cc side valve with detachable head, automatic lubrication, and a Sturmey Archer three-speed gearbox with clutch and kick-start mechanism. The full-spring frame was retained and the brakes were of the contracting band type on both rear and front wheels. The price was £105 solo, and a side-car was available for an additional £30. The price was £10-30 cheaper than most of its competitors, but in spite of all this, by 1923 the company was in trouble with falling sales:

the early success bred an optimism that was not borne out by events. Baker found that the level of post-war sales was much lower than anticipated and could not justify the expansion schemes already completed. He already owed £281,627 to Beardmore Aero Engine Company and, although he still retained the post of managing director, he was busy disinvesting in an attempt to get out with minimum loss.

In an effort to increase the choice of models for the 1923 season, the 350cc two-stroke engine was quietly phased out and greater emphasis placed on the Barr & Stroud engine. At the same time Frank Baker designed a 350cc side-valve four-stroke engine using the same bore and stroke as the Barr & Stroud. The engine had a roller-bearing big end, a built-up crankshaft and an outside fly wheel. The springing of the front forks was also changed and consisted of only one-leaf spring, the top half of the system being replaced by a steel pressing. The rear wheel was unsprung, the frame being the conventional rigid type. Care was taken to point out that these changes were made as a direct result of experience gained in the TT races. To complete the range, the 4½hp 500cc SV engine was offered, and to cater for the low price market a two-speed belt driven 350cc was made available at £55.

The 1923 range:

350cc SV spring frame	solo	£ 80
	combination	105
	sports	100
350cc SV rigid frame	solo	75
	combination	100
	sports	95
500cc SV spring frame	solo	70
	sports	90
B & S 350cc rigid frame	solo	73
	touring	90
350cc SV rigid frame three-speed	solo (all chain)	57.10
	combination sports/touring	75
350cc SV rigid frame two-speed belt drive	solo	55

Even this range of machines failed to improve prospects, and the proverbial writing was on the wall.

Beardmore's response was characteristic: 'In defeat, defiance.' A four-valve OHC 350cc engine was designed by Alf Francis in a 'go for glory' attempt to win the 1924 Isle of Man TT race. For some peculiar reason the tappets could be adjusted by the rider while in motion. The mind boggles at the thought of carrying out this exercise while descending the mountain in the TT.

True to Beardmore tradition, the engines were late and insufficiently tested or developed when they were shipped to the Isle of Man. During practice, teething troubles arose and the team switched to 250cc Precision engines.

The 350cc OHC engine with bore and stroke 72mm x 85.5mm was of considerable interest, containing many novel features. The engine was mounted in the frame sloping forward, the overhead camshaft was driven via bevels from the crankshaft, and the vertical drive shaft incorporated a vernier adjustment for timing adjustment. At the cylinder head a further set of bevels transmitted the drive to the camshaft. The valve rockers had roller followers and two operating fingers for the valves, there being two inlet and two exhaust valves housed in a pent-roof combustion chamber. An Amac two-way carburettor (twin choke) was mounted at the end of two long induction pipes in order to obtain a ramming effect.

The vertical camshaft drive shaft was extended up past the camshaft bevel and further bevel gears were used to drive the magneto, which sat on top of the cylinder head parallel to the camshaft and crankshaft axis. This also had a vernier coupling for timing adjustments. The engine was capable of 7000 rev/min. The frame dispensed with the front and rear leaf springs of the touring bike. The Druid-type front fork was of standard pattern using a coil spring; the frame was roughly triangular and provided a very low seating position. The whole concept conformed to the best competition practice and deserved a better fate. But once again there was insufficient planning at the start and too many loose ends at the finish.

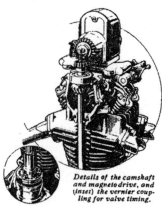

Details of the camshaft and magneto drive, and (inset) the vernier coupling for valve timing.

Beardmore Precision four-valve. (Courtesy of Mitchell Library)

The Precision 250cc engines with a bore and stroke of 59mm x 90mm were also of considerable technical interest. The engine was mounted at an angle sloping forward in the frame, and the cylinder head had two valves operating in a hemispherical head. The valves were push-rod operated and differed from other layouts by being closed by means of a common three-leaf spring. This spring was secured at mid-point to a bridge which spanned the top of the cylinder head. In theory this was indeed a very good arrangement, allowing cooling air around the valve stems. However, in practice the layout caused excessive side thrust which caused rapid wear on the valve guides and resulted in the machines breaking down during the race. Again this was a case of insufficient attention being given to detail and testing.

At Olympia in 1924 Beardmore Precision offered a large range of machines. There was the side-valve 250cc fitted in the leaf-spring frame, and the 250cc OHV engine fitted in the triangular frame with Druid-type front forks. This engine now employed coil springs for the valves and a wickfeed lubrication system for the rocker gear, fed from a separate tank attached to the top of the cylinder head. The four-valve 350cc engine was also offered in a TT-type frame which had the wheel base extended by two inches due to the machine experiencing wheel wobble during the race. Machines of 500cc and 598cc SV were offered with side-cars, and the Barr & Stroud option was maintained.

It was all to no avail, and having offered two-stroke, side valves, sleeve valves, overhead valves, spring frames, rigid frames, chain drive and belt drive, various gearboxes and change-speed mechanism, the fact remained that the machines were not competitive in an overcrowded market. In 1925 the Midland Bank foreclosed.

Precision, when it started, enjoyed a close relationship with Webley and Scott, the gun manufacturers. Webley had manufactured some of Precision's engines in the early days and during World War I. Precision had returned the compliment by manufacturing gun parts for Webley. This liaison carried on after the Beardmore takeover. Colonel Farquhar, a director of Webley, had designed a machine gun in which the Admiralty were interested, and at their urging Beardmore and Webley made a joint effort to manufacture the machine guns at King's Norton. However, the scheme fell through after a great deal of money and effort had been spent, although the reasons for the failure of the gun were not due to any defect in the design. The move was, of course, opposed by Vickers who did not want any competition and who 'had the ear' of the War Office; but the General Army staff were also reluctant to accept anything new. Had this project been successful, it might have carried the firm through the economic depression of the 1920s and into more prosperous times.

The cantilever spring system was expensive and also made the machine heavier than its stablemate 'Dunelt'. In spite of all attempts to be the lowest priced, Dunelt could always beat them. No doubt the burden of debt due to the ill-advised expansion scheme had a lot to do with the problem. The heirs to Beardmore Precision were Dunford & Elliot Ltd, who made the Dunelt motorcycle and who had been in the background since 1917. For the record, Frank Baker restarted and manufactured the Baker two-stroke motorcycle, using Villiers engines. The name 'F. E. Baker' had never been dropped.

DUNELT
MOTORCYCLES

Dunelt motorcycles – novel two-stroke engine

DUNFORD & Elliot Ltd was founded in 1902 in Sheffield and carried on business as iron and steel merchants. In 1907 the company acquired patents for the production of hollow steel rods and bars, and in 1916 it patented improvements on the process used for the manufacture of rock drills and gun and rifle barrels. In 1913, before the onset of World War I, Dunford & Elliot opened a factory in Birmingham for the manufacture of small-diameter gun barrels. In 1917 the company was purchased by Beardmore, although it seems to have been a personal acquisition and, like Arrol-Johnston, was not part of the Beardmore industrial complex.

Beardmore's reason for purchasing the company was the steelmaking and special processes business. He had been involved with the manufacture of the Vickers Maxim machine gun at the Tongland factory, as well as with Webley and Scott, and no doubt the significance of the Dunford & Elliot

TT sports Dunelt. (© Mortons Motorcycle Media Ltd)

hollow-bar process for the manufacture of small-bore gun barrels was not lost on him. The Dunelt motorcycle had not been announced to the public at the time of Beardmore's purchase, but experimental work had been in progress prior to then and Beardmore encouraged its development. He may well have envisaged a company rivalling BSA, thus Dunford & Elliot received Beardmore's full backing and doubtless the novelty of the design appealed to him. The idea of using a double-diameter piston in order to obtain improved scavenging in two-stroke engines was not new, the principal having been employed successfully in large marine and stationary engines. However the application to a small high-speed engine was new.

Dunelt aimed to achieve in the motorcycle world what Henry Ford had achieved in the car industry. The new engine was intended to be an efficient, reasonably powerful, low-cost power unit which, installed in a simple frame, would offer transport for the masses at a popular price. These aims were identical to those of F. E. Baker's Precision company which the Beardmore Aero Engine Company acquired two years later and, as previously mentioned, for reasons never fully explained.

The theory behind the design of the Dunelt engine was that the displacement of a piston in a cylinder is only about 80 per cent of the capacity of the cylinder, thus leaving 20 per cent of dead gas to live charge. A better burned-to-unburned gas ratio was achieved by the use of a double-diameter piston. The piston in the cylinder had a swept volume of 500cc, but the piston drawing the charge into the crankcase and via transfer ports to the working cylinder had a capacity of 770cc. The air trapped between the top of the large diameter part of the piston and the bottom of the working cylinder was transferred to the crankcase by means of a transfer port and did not affect the volumetric efficiency in any way. A certain amount of the new charge may have been lost through the exhaust port, but this loss was made up for by the increased scavenging efficiency.

In 1925 Dunelt entered a 500cc two-stroke for the side-car TT, with the intention of demonstrating that the design could compete with the most advanced four-stroke machines. The engines had detachable aluminium cylinder heads and Duralumin connecting rods with roller big ends. In the event they proved to be both fast and reliable, and the company increased the range by offering a 250cc machine on the same principal. The year 1929 marked the end of the Beardmore era with the sale of his shares, and therefore subsequent models do not fall within the scope of this history.

In 1931 Dunelt ceased the manufacture of their own engines, closed the Birmingham factory, and moved to the steel company's factory in Sheffield where they continued with a 350cc Villiers engine two-stroke. The end of the road for Dunelt came in 1935. The cycle business was discontinued as the expansion of the special steel products division required all available

AN ENGINE "ANALYSED."

DIMPLE IN PISTON CROWN TO CLEAR PLUG POINTS

COMPRESSION SPACE

HOLDING-DOWN BOLT

DIAGRAMMATIC VIEW OF THE PORT POSITIONS AND THE COMPRESSION SPACE WHEN THE PISTON IS AT THE TOP OF ITS STROKE.

TRANSFER PASSAGE

EXHAUST PORTS

INLET PORTS

UNUSUAL RING JOINT

OIL PUMP ON MAGNETO SPINDLE

THE ENGINE IN PART SECTION

DIVIDED WASHERS RETAINING THE BIG END ROLLERS

BALL RACE DRIVE SIDE

BALL RACE TIMING SIDE

BALANCE WEIGHTS

The 249 c.c. DUNELT.

THIS well-known two-stroke engine is unusual and interesting, for it has what is called a "truncated" piston; in other words, the piston has two diameters, the lower one being considerably greater than the upper. The lower part of the cylinder is of correspondingly greater diameter. This results in the crank-case charge being considerably larger than it would be with a piston of the usual type; the engine is, in effect, supercharged. The upper piston ring grooves are formed in a steel band, the remainder of the piston being of aluminium.

THE RECIPROCATING PARTS, IN DETAIL.

'An Engine "Analysed"', *The Motor Cycle*, 1929.

space in the factory. It had the distinction of being the only one of Beardmore's transport ventures to remain solvent throughout its life.

Dunford & Elliot Ltd was sold to the Sheffield steelmakers, Hadfields Ltd. Today, like everything else that formed part of the Beardmore empire, no trace of Dunelt exists, and the site at Attercliffe in Sheffield has now been bulldozed.

J. H. KELLY & COMPANY
AND BEARDMORE'S
COMMERCIAL VEHICLES

J. H. Kelly & Company – back to heavies again –
Chenard Walcker trailer system – use of Meadows engines
in preference to Beardmore's four and six-cylinder diesel engines

THE firm of J. H. Kelly & Company was founded by James Angus in 1851 for the purpose of building farm carts. The firm flourished and between 1858 and 1871 they won awards every year at the Glasgow Agricultural Show. In about 1870 the firm was taken over by J. H. Kelly who had been works manager under James Angus. Kelly branched out into building vans and wagons, achieving success in exporting many of his products to such unlikely places as the Falkland Islands, where some were still in use 50 years after they had been supplied. Kelly specialised in horse-drawn bakers' vans, converting to motor vehicles without any problem. Practically all the major bakery firms in Britain used Kelly vans and some were even supplied to South Africa where, with the advent of the Boer War, Kelly supplied special military horse-drawn wagons on contract to the War Office.

During the military occupation of Germany after World War I, a Scottish soldier reported seeing a baker's van in Cologne, recognisable by the hub caps with the name 'J. H. Kelly Parkhead'.

Kelly was kept busy with motor vehicles and built the first bodies for Albion and Halley. Minerva and Bean were other customers. Even when Beardmore took over in the early 1920s, Kelly continued to build bodies. Not only did he supply outside customers, but he also continued with cartwright work, *ie* the building of carts and other horse-drawn vehicles. Kelly built a large number of taxi bodies and bodies for some of the Anniesland and Coatbridge products. The company was acquired for £10,000 by Beardmore when Kelly retired in 1923.

Arrol-Johnston, of course, had their own body shops at Dumfries. But the Van Street works kept busy even after the Anniesland car had ceased and the taxi works had moved to Hendon. They were still building prototype bodies for Beardmore's various attempts to enter the heavy vehicles market, right up to the outbreak of World War II. The development of factory-built pressed steel bodies made the old wood-framed specialist coachwork an unprofitable business. Kelly built quality coachwork, but the company never really got beyond the stage of being a local builder. It had always been a profitable business, but it was financially hamstrung by Beardmore's eccentric financial policies – he frequently used the assets of one company to guarantee the overdraft of another less-solvent company. Kelly was therefore denied the capital necessary for expansion. With the collapse of the Scottish motor industry and the disintegration of the Beardmore empire, J. H. Kelly & Company simply faded away.

In 1929 William Beardmore & Company Ltd formed a separate commercial vehicle department to manage the Van Street works at Parkhead and to acquire the British manufacturing rights of Chenard-Walcker, the successful French multi-wheeler, heavy-haulage tractor and trailer. It was intended to build these at Parkhead and no doubt fit them with Beardmore diesel engines. However, because of various difficulties, the main move was not made and the tractors and trailers were assembled at a factory at Clapham in London.

Three models were developed – the 'Anaconda', 'Python' and 'Cobra' – and put on the market in 1931. The 'Anaconda' was the largest with 15-ton loading and a 115hp 'Meadows' engine; the 'Python' was 10 to 15-ton axle-loading with 95hp engine; and the 'Cobra' 10-ton axle-loading and 50hp engine, also 'Meadows'. The design incorporated an ingenious load-sharing device so that a portion of the load from the four-wheeled trailer was transferred to the rear wheels of the tractor, thus incorporating the mobility of the trailer with the load-carrying capacity of an articulated vehicle.

The design was well received by the trade press, but only a few vehicles were sold. The timing of the venture had been wrong: it was during the depression of the late 1920s and early '30s.

At least one Cobra still exists, fully restored thanks to the foresight of Messrs Marks and Spencer who sponsored the rebuilding of a derelict vehicle discovered by Nick Baldwin, a well-known figure in the motor trade and restoration business who lived near Yarmouth. In the meantime the Van Street works continued to build the occasional lorry and bus fitted with Beardmore high-speed diesel engines, but they were unprofitable and did not get past the prototype stage. The Chenard-Walcker business was sold in 1932 to the newly-formed Multi-Wheelers Company Ltd. Van Street works again discussed the formation of a commercial vehicle business, but lack of capital ruled otherwise.

TRANSPORT
IN THE AIR

Beardmore acting mainly as subcontractor – development of the 'Inflexible' – engines for the ill-fated R101 airship – the world's first flush-deck aircraft carrier

DURING World War I Beardmore built prototype fighter and trainer aeroplanes based on the designs of DFW of Germany. The 'WB' III was the only one to enter service, but it was not particularly notable. It was a 'Sopwith Pup' with folding wings. The factory at Inchinnan produced a variety of aircraft as sub-contractors. These included RAF BE2C, 'Sopwith Pup' and 'Camel Wight' 840 sea planes, and Nieuport 12 and Handley Page four-engined bombers. They also designed and built two 'WB' XXVI two-seater fighter planes for the Latvian government. Armament consisted of three Farquhar machine guns and the planes were fitted with Rolls-Royce 'Eagle' IX engines, with a speed of 145mph. Despite passing all its acceptance tests, no contract for manufacture was received. In 1912 Beardmore anticipated the idea of aircraft carriers by recommending to the Admiralty that they build a ship to carry and launch sea planes. Winston Churchill, as First Sea Lord, rejected the idea. Nevertheless, Beardmore Company Dalmuir designed and built the world's first flush-deck aircraft carrier, the 'Argus', commissioned in

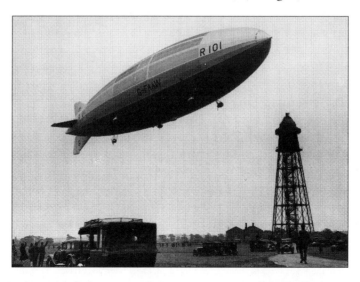

The R101 airship. (Courtesy of Museum of Flight, National Museums of Scotland)

1918. The aircraft factory was closed but re-opened in 1924. Beardmore had already obtained the manufacturing rights of the Rorbach all-metal construction system, and he succeeded in interesting the Air Ministry in the building of a very large monoplane. Beardmore, far ahead as usual, had ideas of conversion to passenger use, a concept probably 20 years ahead of its time.

The 'Inflexible', as it was called, was the largest land aeroplane ever built in the world at that time (see page 93). It had a wingspan of 156 feet 7 inches and was 82 feet 9 inches long. Powered by three Rolls-Royce 650hp 'Condor' V12 engines, it had a designed speed of 104mph and the undercarriage wheels were eight feet in diameter.

According to Ian Johnston's book *Beardmore Built*, some parts of the aeroplane were built in Holland, but according to reports from Dalmuir the entire aeroplane was built in Scotland. Not only that, but the aircraft designer W. S. Shackleton created another aeroplane almost as large – the 'Inverness' – a seaplane with a wingspan of 96 feet 9 inches, 54 feet long with two 450hp Napier 'Lions' engines. The 'Inverness', however, was not successful and was probably underpowered.

There was a worry when the 'Inflexible' was reassembled at Martlesham that the runway would not be long enough and it was duly extended. This turned out to be unnecessary as the 'Inflexible', with Squadron Leader Jack Noakes at the controls, took off very easily with only a short run. Later tests carrying maximum load were not so impressive. The aeroplane, being underpowered, had a long shallow climb that proved to be a bit of a 'nail biter'. The RAF nicknamed it the Beardmore 'Impossible'; nevertheless it made several public appearances, including the air display at Hendon.

The Air Ministry foresaw the need to build aircraft using light, high-duty metal. The old wooden construction covered with doped canvas was unable to cope with new developments and more powerful engines (the De Havilland Mosquito was a wooden construction but used modern glues and different methods).

The Air Ministry regarded the 'Inflexible' as purely experimental; it was used for the investigation of metal corrosion due to atmospheric conditions and metal fatigue caused by repeated stress reversals.

Beardmore, on the other hand, foresaw the use of large aircraft as passenger carriers. The R101 disaster* proved him right.

Another non-starter was the 'WB' VIII. This was a triplane with two fuselages on a central engine nacelle. Each fuselage carried twelve passengers and one crew member, whilst the central nacelle carried the pilot, navigator

---

* The cause of the R101 crash has never been identified. There were no survivors. One theory is that the forward gas bags leaked causing the craft to become nose heavy. Another is that due to the power limitations on the propellers, the craft was unable to gain sufficient height.

and engineer and three Galloway 'Atlantic' V12 engines. One engine was a 'pusher' and the other two drove traction propellers via shaft drives.

Another short-lived venture was the 'Bennie' Railplane. This consisted of an aerodynamically-shaped passenger compartment with an airscrew at each end, designed to be suspended from a single overhead rail. A single overhead track 426 yards long was erected for test purposes, but the dream of a high-speed connection between Glasgow and Edinburgh came to nothing.

Beardmore also built several airships, of which the R34 was the most famous, being in 1919 the first airship to fly the Atlantic, making a double crossing. With few military contracts available he experimented with a small single-seat monoplane using the two-cylinder opposed, air-cooled Bristol Cherub. The aeroplane, using Beardmore's initials, was called the 'Wee Bee I'. Despite winning several competitions, it failed to find a niche in the market. In 1924 the British government decided to build large commercial airships. One, the R100, was to be built by private enterprise; the other, the R101, was government-sponsored on a 'cost no object' basis.

The airships were a bold concept, visualising a transport system that would span the world and consolidate the British Empire. In the event it turned out to be a 'boffin's paradise'. In the case of the R101 almost every scientist of note had a hand in the design, and mechanical curiosities, all with their own built-in weight penalties, abounded. It was decided at the outset that diesel engines should be used. It was calculated that the lower fuel consumption would show a saving in weight of fuel carried, which would more than offset any increase in weight of the engines. Diesel fuel was also considered to be less of a safety hazard. In actual fact the engines and the propellers were three times as heavy as an equivalent petrol engine and prop. The diminished fire hazard, with all that hydrogen in proximity, was tragically irrelevant.

Not much information is readily available on Allan Chorlton. He was, however, a very brilliant engineer with an international reputation outside Britain. He had been invited by leading engineering and automobile societies in America to present technical papers on engine design. Under his guidance, William Beardmore & Company was recognised as the leading high-speed diesel manufacturer in Britain and possibly Europe and it was on this reputation that Beardmore was chosen to supply the high-speed diesels for the R101 airship project.

Allan Chorlton came to Beardmore from Ruston and Hornsby. To his credit he had already designed several successful diesels, including a large 'Vee' formation engine for submarines in 1919 which ran at the then high speed of 550 rev/min. Chorlton was a very versatile engineer; not only did he design engines but also airframes. Successful engines included the 'Typhoon' and the 'Simoon'. Both of these engines were eight-in-line; the Typhoon was a diesel while the Simoon was petrol-fuelled. Chorlton was also the trustee of certain Italian patents on oil engines and received royalties from Beardmore on all engines produced by them and built to his designs from 1918 onwards. He also invented a very successful fuel-injection system. Chorlton retired from the engineering profession to become a Member of Parliament, an extraordinary change of profession.

The Royal Aircraft Establishment at Farnborough was also active in the development of high-speed diesel engines and had a single-cylinder test unit 8 inch bore x 11 inch stroke, running at 1100 rev/min. In fact many modifications to the Beardmore 'Tornado' engines were carried out at Farnborough under the guidance of Lieutenant Commander Cave-Brown-Cave. The 'Tornado' engines destined for the R101 were eight-in-line, $8\frac{1}{4}$ inch bore x 12 inch stroke, rated at 585bhp continuous cruising at 900 rev/min with 650hp maximum. These engines, although rather heavier than the original estimate, largely due to having to use a heavier crankshaft on account of torsional vibrations, were satisfactory and were not, as most historians claim, unreliable. The entire trouble lay in the fact that the engine characteristics did not match the propellers. Eight-in-line engines do produce torsional vibrations and the propellers were totally unable to cope with this.

Originally the propellers were designed to be reversible, but this refinement had to be abandoned in favour of fixed, solid blades. Lanchester dampers on the engine and a spring-drive hub added weight without solving the problem. In the end the engines had to be derated and even then the propellers were unreliable. The problem with the propellers was a metallurgical one: there was no suitable blade material available at that time. Perhaps the problem would have been less severe with, for example, a V12 engine, but Beardmore cannot be blamed for building an engine similar to previous successful engines, and the 'Tornado' was used successfully in subsequent rail car applications. Beardmore later developed a twelve-cylinder horizontally opposed diesel engine 6 inch bore x $6\frac{1}{2}$ inch stroke, 505bhp at 1750 rev/min, and which was almost half the weight of the 'Tornado'.

Before the ill-fated flight to India, my father visited Cardington where the R101 airship was being built. Having climbed all round it, he commented on the close proximity of the enlarged gas bags to the frame, sometimes separated from a spar by a piece of rubber padding. He wisely declined the invitation to go on one of the trial flights. The whole project was three years late in taking to the air and even then it was an appalling act of folly. Nothing was ready for its maiden flight to India, which had been brought forward for political reasons.

As a result of the R101 disaster, the national airship building programme was cancelled, the airship building division of Beardmore was closed down, and the development of high-speed diesel engines was curtailed.

THE FALL OF
WILLIAM BEARDMORE
& COMPANY LTD

THE BEGINNING OF THE END

The London Road engine works – the wreckers – H M Treasury accountants

THE London Road engine works was the site of Beardmore's major expansion at the turn of the century and, along with Duncan Stewart Ltd, was well established as manufacturers of steam engines for cotton mills, sugar mills and marine use. It was here that Beardmore built the Stewart steam wagon. In the years before 1914 he had built up a large, prosperous business by obtaining manufacturing licences from companies in Britain and Europe which gave him technical expertise equal to any other engineering company in Britain. Some of these agreements did, however, turn out to be more of a liability than an advantage.

By the late 1920s the British shipbuilding industry had been in dire straits for some time and the marine diesel division suffered from a lack of orders. The aircraft engine company was badly hit by the R101 disaster but went on to develop successful high-speed diesels for rail cars, *etc.* The railway locomotive business was in steep decline, so the only remaining product applicable to road transport was the high-speed diesel for commercial vehicles. The range consisted of a four-cylinder 65hp and a six-cylinder 100hp. These engines shared a common bore and stroke. Beardmore diesels were fitted in various bus and truck chassis such as Halley. Albion Motors

The 'Inflexible', 1929.

supplied 30 chassis with Beardmore engines to the Glasgow corporation in 1935, and in 1936 Beardmore produced a 7½-ton commercial vehicle chassis with their 5579cc four-cylinder direct injection oil engine. At the same time they announced their intention to produce a complete range of vehicles to include the four and six-cylinder engines consisting of the 7½-ton four-wheel chassis, a 13-ton six wheeler, a 15-ton rigid eight wheeler, and well as single and double-deck passenger chassis. Nothing further was heard of this scheme and with it died the last remaining trace of the Beardmore transport saga.

Beardmore never achieved the racing or commercial successes he so strongly desired and, sadly, he has never been given the recognition he deserved as a pioneer, patron and enthusiastic supporter of motorsport. All great endeavours need a bit of luck to achieve success. Beardmore was conspicuously unlucky. He had far-reaching vision and many of his ideas were ahead of his time, but his almost naïve lack of business skills laid him open for almost everyone to take advantage of him. Perhaps, and in many ways, Beardmore was too much of a gentleman.

A serious financial crisis arose in 1926 when Vickers, who had concluded a satisfactory deal with Armstrong-Whitworth, decided to dissolve their amalgamation with William Beardmore & Company. Beardmore was able to buy the Vickers holding using his wife's private fortune, but the action started the alarm bells ringing among Beardmore's creditors, mainly the Bank of England and H M Treasury, who appointed Sir William McLintock to carry out an examination of the company. McLintock's report was a devastating condemnation of Beardmore's style of management, and the company was shown to be virtually bankrupt. The creditors appointed a committee to investigate the situation in 1927 and by 1928 Beardmore had been removed from all executive duties and banished to his office at Duncan Stewart Ltd, possibly one of the only managing directors and major shareholders ever banned from entering his own works.

Strictly speaking, developments in the heavy vehicle market and high-speed diesels after 1928 should not be attributed to Beardmore, but the impetus of the pattern set under his control carried on for the next ten years without much alteration to his original policies. The chairmanship of the company was taken over by Beardmore's nephew Val Stewart, son of Marie Beardmore and Duncan Stewart. Val Stewart, although a director, never took an active role in the management of the Beardmore company.

Enter the wreckers. When Vickers pulled the financial rug from under Beardmore's feet and the Bank of England's receiver, Sir Montagu Norman, took control, Beardmore was forced to retire to his office at Duncan Stewart Ltd. From there he watched the dismemberment of his empire with anger and frustration, and not without reason. It is debatable whether

Lord Invernairn
at the end of his tragic saga.

the accountancy fraternity are best qualified to control the destiny of a high-technology industry. Norman's men were more concerned with liquidating the Treasury loans than with creating a viable engineering industry. Consequently many of Beardmore's less tangible assets which did not appear to be of immediate cash value, or had been loss-makers by reason of bad management, were ignored. Many people felt that by gathering together all the businesses under a single management structure, with a common manufacturing base, and distributing overhead charges equitably, a viable engineering giant consisting of the light car, the taxi business, aero engines and high-speed diesels, *etc* could have been created. Sadly, such an imaginative scheme was scarcely considered by the accountants.

In 1928 a Canadian efficiency expert, Walter Ord, was called in. He closed down the locomotive works in the middle of a contract for the Belgian government, paying breach of contract damages rather than continue to make losses. The Napier shipyard was sold and dismantled. Both locomotive building and shipbuilding were suffering a worldwide recession and their closure was long overdue. One by one the loss-makers disappeared. The remaining industries, as pointed out, were not really viable as separate entities and eventually Parkhead Forge★ remained the only solvent enterprise of a once great empire. After completion of his contract with William Beardmore & Company, Ord moved to the Hillman Motor Company where, with the help of the newly-designed 'Minx', the company survived long enough to join up with Humber.

When William Beardmore died in 1936 the financial affairs of his estate were so complicated that it took three years to sort them out.

★ The site occupied by Parkhead Forge now accommodates a supermarket, appropriately named 'The Forge'.

BIBLIOGRAPHY

Book and journal publications referred to in this book include:

Baldwin, Nick: 'Bringing the Beardmore Back to Life' in *Vintage Commercial Vehicle Magazine* (*c.*1985).

Boddy, W: 'Fragments of Forgotten Makes' in *Motor Sport* (Aries Press).

Brearley, Harry: *Stainless Pioneer* (Sheffield: British Steel/Kelham Island Industrial Museum, 1989).

Clark, Ronald H: *The English Steam Wagon* (Norwich: Goose & Sons Ltd, 1960).

Gunston, Bill: *World Encyclopaedia of Aero Engines*.

Johnston, Ian: *Beardmore Built* (Clydebank District Libraries and Museum department: 1993).

Macdonald, Craig and A. S. E. Browning: 'History of the Motor Industry in Scotland' in *Proceedings of the Institute of Mechanical Engineering* (1960-61).

Morgan, Nick: *Enterprise and Industry*.

Moss, Michael S. and John R. Hume: *Beardmore, The History of a Scottish Industrial Giant* (Glasgow: Glasgow University, 1977).

Moss, Michael S. and Alison Turton: *The Bitter with the Sweet* (Glasgow: Fletcher and Stewart Limited, 1988).

Oliver, George: *Motor Trials and Tribulations* (Edinburgh: Her Majesty's Stationery Office and Glasgow Museums, 1993).

Worthington Williams, M.: *The Scottish Motor Industry* (Shire Publications Limited, 1989).

Magazine publications referred to include:

The Autocar (London: Illiffe & Sons)
Automobile (Surrey: Enthusiast Publishing Limited)
The Automotor Journal
The Beardmore News
The Car
The Commercial Motor
The Classic Motor Cycle (Peterborough: E.M.A.P. National Publications Limited)
The Motor Cycle
Motor Cycling
Motor Sport
The Motor Transport – Motor World